Practical Woodca
Design & Application

James E. Seitz, Ph.D.

Schiffer Publishing Ltd

4880 Lower Valley Road, Atglen, PA 19310 USA

Dedication

To those striving to become true artisans in the design and carving of useful products.

Published by Schiffer Publishing Ltd.
4880 Lower Valley Road
Atglen, PA 19310
Phone: (610) 593-1777; Fax: (610) 593-2002
E-mail: Schifferbk@aol.com
Please visit our web site catalog at **www.schifferbooks.com**
We are always looking for people to write books on new and related subjects. If you have an idea for a book please contact us at the above address.

This book may be purchased from the publisher.
Include $3.95 for shipping.
Please try your bookstore first.
You may write for a free catalog.

In Europe, Schiffer books are distributed by
Bushwood Books
6 Marksbury Ave.
Kew Gardens
Surrey TW9 4JF England
Phone: 44 (0)20-8392-8585
Fax: 44 (0)20-8392-9876
E-mail: Bushwd@aol.com
Free postage in the UK. Europe: air mail at cost

Copyright © 2003 by James E. Seitz
Library of Congress Control Number: 2002114156

Designed by Mark David Bowyer
Type set in Americana XBd BT/Lydian BT

ISBN: 0-7643-1690-7
Printed in China

Contents

Acknowledgments

Credit for assisting in the development of this book goes to many individuals. Grateful acknowledgement is hereby extended to Ted Gerhart of Gerhart Studios (carved business signs), Ralph Moeller (carved door and mantel), Florencio Reyes, M.D. (carved office sign), and Donald Wheeler (carved brooches and bolo tie) for providing photos or permitting me to photograph their work for inclusion in this book. Additional expressions of appreciation are extended to my wife, Arlene, for her assistance in countless ways, to my grandson, Jackson, for his photographic work, to the staff at Schiffer Publishing, especially Jeff Snyder for editorial advice, and to countless others whose assistance and influence over the years continue to find fruition in my work. Their gracious assistance has contributed substantially.

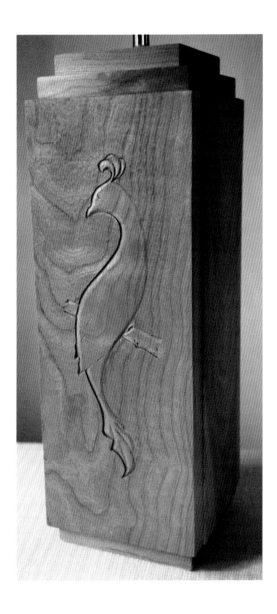

Introduction

Woodcarvers at different levels of development can benefit from this book. Consider yourself among them if you are just beginning to carve wood or have progressed to an advanced position in the field. Even if you have become expert, you will find much of the material on design and its application to useful products to be new and informative. Any preference you may have for a particular type of carving is also likely to be addressed within the broad array of applications presented throughout the text. Moreover, the principles of esthetics and product design described apply with few restrictions to all types of carving.

Both the commonly practiced and unusual variations of relief carving and incising are covered. Among these are well-known practices, such as chip carving, bas-relief, bold relief, and figure whittling, as well as less-frequently employed practices in coelanaglyphic carving, intaglio, and beveled-edge carving. Persons accustomed to carving figures in the round, in particular, may be amazed to discover the many ways their woodcarvings can be made to assist in the performance of useful work. No longer need the figures be made only for display or conversational purposes.

Written by an experienced woodcarver, designer, and author, the text is presented in easy-to-follow language and contains numerous illustrations and examples. Important rules of design are amply explained and applied, with over 200 photographs and 70 drawings and patterns supplementing the written material. A total of 155 different products are portrayed. Each product is either decorated by carving or formed completely by it, and all are practical, in that, they assist in some way in the performance of work. Chests, property signs, wall shelves, and footstools are among the items embellished by carving. Examples of items shaped by carving include nut bowls, spatulas, place-card holders, and coin banks, to name a few. The depth and variety of coverage is truly extensive. Woodcarvers, by and large, will find the material is replete with ideas of what to create and how to go about individualizing that next gift or item for use in and about the home.

Individuals who know how to construct the articles which they intend to decorate can do the work when and as they please. This would seem to be a distinct advantage over purchasing manufactured items. Although the techniques of construction are not the main focus of this publication, primarily because of limitations in space, any knowledgeable woodcarver who has not already learned woodworking practices should be able to master the fundamentals by referring to a book on the subject. Photographs and dimensions of completed articles are given in this book for those desiring and able to duplicate some of the work. A few techniques of carving are illustrated, but that area of the practice is not extensively detailed either. The reader is expected to be familiar with the rudiments of carving and the safe and proper use of tools in order to put the information into practice as presented.

The emphasis throughout is on design and its application. This area of endeavor constitutes a field which, based on the author's observation, has been largely neglected. The insecurity attendant to the uncertainty involved may be the reason. Designing is creating, and creating deals in the unknown. Seldom, as a consequence, will every observer be appreciative of an outcome. Woodcarvers are no exception.

Designing is definitely an art. Were that not so, one could simply consult a list of formulas and apply them in a consistent, methodical way. As it is, the process gives quarter to many possibilities and interpretations with each shaping of an object or arranging of a decoration. Matters of balance, harmony, variety, symmetry, coherence, and so forth are too vague or elusive for some persons to venture into the field. Even in product design, where physical laws sometimes prevail, there exits many opportunities to err. That, undoubtedly, contributes to the reason many woodcarvers continue to copy their work.

While designing is not easy, it can be learned and applied by practically anyone who makes a concerted effort. You actually might find the practices to be easier to follow than first anticipated. Armed with this book, a personal commitment, and a creative bent, you will have the wherewithal to begin designing on your own. Nurture that creative ability. It is essential in design, and design, in turn, is an essential component for progressing from a position of craftsmanship in woodcarving to one of artisanship.

Chapter One
Purposes of Carving Wood

Articles of wood may be simply divided into those made for a practical purpose and those which are not. Practical articles are designed for doing work or for assisting in the performance of work. This designation distinguishes items such as stools and bowls from pieces functioning strictly for some decorative or symbolic purpose. Oil paintings, religious statues, and carved caricatures are among the objects intended to serve a purpose other than some physical activity. They appeal primarily to the senses and emotions.

This differentiation does not mean that practical items, all of which serve a utilitarian purpose, cannot be made artistic. Surely they can be, and carving is a way to enhance them. The use intended largely determines the form of an item's design and its manner of application. There are several possibilities in this regard.

Decoration

A primary purpose of carving is decoration. Although fireplace mantels, writing desks, jewelry boxes, and a host of other articles will function usefully without being decorated, the addition of effectively executed relief carvings or incised designs in suitable areas can provide the special, artistic touch needed. Carved embellishments of this kind seldom aid in the performance of work. Most are intended to beautify, nothing more.

A form of decorative carving adorns the slanted surface of the cherry-wood desk shown in Figure 1.1. The incised design appears close-up in Figure 1.2. Unobtrusively designed, the carving serves the sole purpose of providing a unique point of interest on an otherwise plain surface. Imagine the appearance without it.

Simplicity of design is often to be preferred, regardless of the method of application. An important analysis consists of whether or not a scheme seems overdone. Novices occasionally overlook this matter. They become engrossed in technique when learning. Perfecting skill becomes a dominant concern for some, and as a consequence, elaborate carving may occur at the expense of good design. The overdecorated, gaudy items that sometimes result can be even more displeasing than if they had been left plain, for no amount of cleverness in tooling and construction will compensate for superfluous design.

Figure 1.1. Much of the effectiveness of the incised floral decoration on this cherry-wood desk is due to its simplicity and placement.

Figure 1.2. The unconventionally balanced distribution of details contributes to the design's uniqueness.

Utility

The second basic purpose of carving is the creation of useful objects. In other words, an object receives its shape through carving. Sawing along an outline on the wood might precede the act of carving, but the final form results from the use of carving tools. While the finished configuration should be pleasing to the eye, the primary object driving the design of the article is its utility.

Hand-carved wooden ladles, paper knives, and nut bowls are examples of items whose use is the main concern. They may be made austere and plain, or they may be designed with attention to esthetic principles. A rule in the common language of product design commands: *If the item works well but doesn't look good, change it!*

By way of illustrating this aspect of design, consider the hand-carved redwood dipper pictured in Figure 1.3. It is designed for the specific purpose of lifting water from a bucket in a sauna and dispersing the contents over heated stones. Its shape is the result of the designer-carver's effort to achieve this function effectively. Thus, evidence can be seen of attention having been given to both utility and esthetics.

Does the dipper satisfy the important design criteria? As to practical function, it does. It can be handily filled with water in the amount desired, seldom necessitates use of a second hand for tipping the bucket while dipping, provides for easily holding the handle without slipping, allows the hand to remain clear of scalding steam rising from the heater while pouring, and can be stored in the bucket or suspended from a wall-mounted bracket when not in use. The species of wood forming the dipper also has sufficient durability, yet does not absorb heat excessively. These criteria are the fundamental bases for judging the dipper's usefulness. Of course, solutions to problems of utility alone can take more than one form.

Esthetic considerations are another matter. The form, color, and arrangement of components of an article define artistic merit. The dipper has favorable qualities. The small scroll on the handle's end is strictly a decorative device for terminating the piece. The parabolic cup and subtly shaped handle exhibit flowing curves and a much smoother transition of lines than would be possible with an assembly made of a plain, though usable, cylindrical cup on the end of a straight stick. Also, two coats of exterior grade polyurethane protect the redwood from absorbing water and eventually discoloring. Evidence exists of attention having been given to meeting all-important criteria.

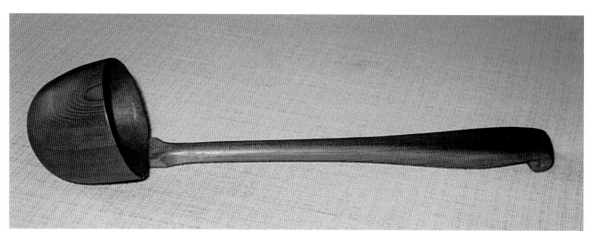

Figure 1.3. This redwood dipper represents a class of articles in which design and carving combine to produce utilitarian form.

Decoration and Utility

A third purpose of carving wooden items, which may be thought of as a combination of the previous purposes, provides for varying degrees of utility and adornment. It follows neither of the extremes explained previously. For example, consider the round handle of a letter opener or that of a walking stick. A carving about the spot of holding will effectively aid in gripping by eliminating any smoothness present. The carved configuration can then serve both a useful purpose when gripping by hand and an artistic purpose at other times. Unlike strictly decorative carvings, it provides some utilitarian value, but unlike some practical objects, it serves only part of an article's utility. The tooling directly affects the appearance and usefulness of the handgrip, only.

The bead-and-ball design along the edges of the knife rack in Figure 1.4 further illustrates the dual purpose. This distinctive form, while decorative, covers spots where it will assist when grasping, lifting, and moving the object. Although the edge-carving's utilitarian value may be slight in comparison to the article's main purpose, it is nonetheless consequential. The same carving placed a distance away from the edges would not have a similar effect. The carving would then be entirely decorative in purpose.

Figure 1.4. On a small, movable article, decorative carvings can often be placed where they will also aid when gripping.

The carved features on the knife rack have been intentionally restricted, for two reasons: First, they were designed to serve the practical purpose mentioned above and, second, the beautiful grain of the butternut wood was not to be obliterated. The intent was to create a useful enhancement, not an overbearing detraction.

Relatively common today are figures carved in full relief. These are the three-dimensional shapes often called "carvings in the round." They occupy more space at public shows than any other form of the craft. Apparently, many craftsmen whittle objects in the round for the joy of carving and to prompt discussion or gain admiration. Occasionally, one will impart some work-related application to his characters. His is an exceptional practice from which others might benefit.

While some carvings in the round are too delicate or are otherwise inappropriate for practical application, a creative mind will relish in developing utilitarian applications for three-dimensional figures. An active imagination is the key. The possibilities are considerable. An Uncle Sam carved for holding letters, a whittled bear nestling a handful of pencils for use at a student's desk, a caricature leaning against the upright ends of a bookrack, and a floral design shaped into a paperweight are a few suggestions. Or, how about an appropriately attired statue carved to hold and dispense announcements while standing at the entrance of a local club's meeting room? Chess pieces, doorstops, and letter knives are other ideas for producing carvings in the round with attendant utility.

A small piece applied as suggested is shown in Figure 1.5. Utility derives from the figure's stability and the narrow saw cut for holding a place-card at the dinner table. The figure's size and position are the result of analyzing the purpose involved. Unlike many ordinary whittlings, this one is merely an adaptation of a decorative piece to a useful purpose. Children, especially, like it.

Figure 1.5. While most whittled figures are made only for display and conversation, one designed for holding a place-card serves an additional purpose.

What other figures could be used instead of a small bunny? Anyone who has fashioned a figure or two in wood can probably develop several workable ideas. Human, animal, floral, and inanimate forms of great variety are within the realm of possibility. Virtually any figure that can be sized and shaped for holding a name-card upright can be adapted to the task, although characters imparting a bit of humor or displaying another relevant feature might be most favorably received. A complete setting of such figures around a table could be a source of lively conversation among guests.

A place-card holder and its finish should be durable, because each piece will be handled and cleaned on occasion. A coating of satin polyurethane will do. This is a practice to observe with most whittlings, whether colored or left unpainted.

The several items shown in this chapter represent only a small part of the variety available for adoption or modification to satisfy individual requirements. Numerous illustrations of other attractive utilitarian applications are included in the chapters that follow. They, too, may be altered to suit or be copied as given.

Chapter Two
Principles and Procedures

Whether a carving is to be decorative or become an integral part of an item's form, the best results are likely to be achieved through planning. Sketching has an important place in the process, and there are important principles of design and construction to be taken into account. A carving's features, such as its size, shape, style, placement, and balance, are then most certain to reach the level of enhancement desired.

Design Considerations

A frequently repeated principle to observe in design is that *form follows function.* To be in keeping with this important rule, an article's shape and appearance must remain secondary to the item's purpose and should not detract from it. An article can function properly only if it does what it is supposed to do without interference by any of the parts. A violation of this guideline may be realized in the case of a picture frame that does not fit as intended, say, by covering huge areas of the painting far from the edges. Footstools made too tall to be stepped onto easily

and the handles of scoops made weak by being carved too thin suggest other problems.

The chances of erring in product design are manifold. Just as a picture frame might not be fitting in size and shape, it can detract in another way from the artwork it is supposed to enhance. An overbearing visual impact could be the problem. The carved, gilded frames commonly placed about paintings during the Victorian period are a case in point. Their size and ornateness seem always to overshadow the pictures they are supposed to enhance. Current standards call for less ostentatious framing.

In several places throughout the world, some work will still be overdone to the point of being gaudy. An example may be seen in the imported trivet shown in Figure 2.1. Although the leaves in the corners and the rosette in the center are acceptable to the eye, the details carved elsewhere appear to be excessive in quantity, irregular in form, and inartistically executed, perhaps, as a result of the maker's concept of design and the use of primitive tools.

Figure 2.1. Lavish detailing and, perhaps, the use of primitive tools have affected the quality of the imported trivet pictured here.

In addition to simplicity and neatness in the carving of practical objects, there is importance in observing the principle of compatibility. When decorating a surface, the design should fit harmoniously within the area being tooled. The outlines of the two must not conflict. To put it another way, a round outline in a square surface, or vice versa, should be avoided.

Corner fillers can be used to fit an otherwise inharmonious shape to a surface. Figure 2.2 shows a means of achieving close harmony between a decoration and the surrounding surface. Corner fillers are not always needed, but their use will produce desirable results in some centrally positioned applications if (1) their style is consistent with that of the central figure and (2) they result in better conformity with the article's shape. The design's outline resulting from such an application should also produce visual order within the decoration.

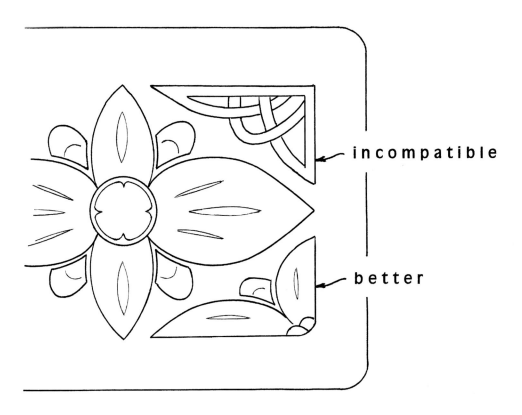

Figure 2.2. Corner fillers of compatible design are sometimes used to provide a close fit between a decorative design and the area decorated.

While corner fillers are useful in certain situations, equally effective results will often be obtained by using directly conforming outlines. The small box in Figure 2.3 illustrates this point. Harmony between the design and the box results primarily from the compatibility of rectangular shapes. The principle involved is both simple and effective.

Figure 2.3. The shape given to this stylized carving's outline illustrates another way to achieve harmony between an article and its decoration.

The decoration on the box's lid is a stylized floral design. What it represents in a general way seems evident, but the fact that it does not exactly duplicate anything real is the legitimate license of the designer. Prominence is achieved by slightly recessing the background of the design, which allows the central figure to stand in a moderately elevated position of relief on the thin wood. Insofar as possible, such matters are taken into account prior to the actual shaping.

On horizontally positioned surfaces, a margin of similar size and symmetry all around the design will generally provide the balanced effect we humans have come to expect. Vertical surfaces usually require a slightly different treatment in order to be visually pleasing. Optical centering comes into play. In vertical applications, the optical center falls at a point slightly above true center, and attention to it in carving results in a larger margin at the bottom than at the top and sides. Symmetrical designs seem to be most affected. Many carved patterns appear to rest below the mid-point of vertical surfaces if made with equal margins all around. The optically pleasing position is determined visually according to the size and composition of the design.

Unlike symmetrical woodcarvings, however, rectangular paintings and photographs of scenes and subjects in non-geometric distribution will occasionally be given borders of similar width all around. Some pictures made for hanging are now framed that way. This practice seems to be imposed by framers and those cutting mats for their convenience, rather than the desire of the artists. For best effect, the principal subjects in the various works are not ordinarily placed in the geometric center.

Consistency is another important consideration at the outset. The indiscriminate mixing of methods of carving can be as unpleasant as anything. A large central figure in relief will clash vividly with a border of boldly incised figures. The two forms seem to confuse the visual senses when placed side-by-side. The recommended practice, for all but a few applications of limited scope, is to use the same method of carving throughout. Lettered objects constitute a legitimate exception to this general rule.

The indiscriminate mixing of design motifs can be disconcerting, also. Geometric figures, for instance, set near an area of realistically styled flowers provide a case in point. Coherence in style must be observed. When making a representational figure, the general practice is to keep the entire design representational. If forming a conventionalized part, the conventionalized style would preferably be continued throughout. Similarly, abstractions do not readily fit within naturalistically styled carvings. And so forth. The possibilities of creating a poor design far outweigh the chances of developing a good one when attempting to combine styles.

As to placement, decorative carvings serve best if cut into surfaces that remain visible where normally positioned. Top and front areas are appropriate spots on boxes and small chests. The sides may also be decorated sparingly, if readily viewed. However, any spot selected must not be subject to excessive wear or probable damage. These considerations restrict the placement of a relief carving to the front panel of a chest made for holding blankets—never across its top upon which a person might sit or on the sides that will likely be hidden in some way. By the same token, a thinly carved, fragile element that could be easily broken has no place at all on a utilitarian piece.

Many of these principles involve little more than simple logic. Others are comparatively complex. Mass, unity, proportion, symmetry, and balance are among the more demanding concerns. Their importance in design and construction must not be ignored.

Balance, Variety, and Perspective

One of the principal ways to achieve balance in design is through symmetry. Although exact symmetry does not often occur in nature (close inspection of animals, plants, and minerals usually reveals differences, even in halves that first appear to be similar), the human eye desires and is accustomed to seeing objects made precisely symmetrical. Evidence of this can be observed in the way we construct dining tables with halves balanced about centerlines and even in the way we arrange chairs in uniform patterns about our tables. Chairs, cabinets, shelves, and numerous other man-made objects customarily display such formal balance.

Symmetrical arrangements are totally acceptable in woodcarving, and they are often preferred because of the visual correspondence and equilibrium the opposing parts provide. The carved box illustrated in this chapter (Figure 2.3) contains an application of one kind. The carving is symmetrically quadrantal, being an exact duplication of halves reversed about two right-angled axes. Its compatibility to the box derives somewhat from the shapes being similarly symmetrical, in addition to the rectangularity involved. Several varieties of symmetrical form are included in Figure 2.4.

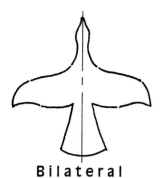

Bilateral

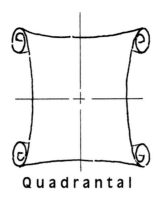

Quadrantal

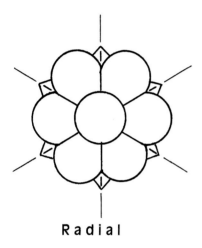

Radial

Asymmetric

Figure 2.4. Figures in bilateral, quadrantal, and radial symmetry balance inherently, but balance in asymmetric forms must be created.

Symmetry necessitates care in positioning and sizing elements on opposite sides of a midpoint. Irregularities from one side to the next will often stand out. To avoid this, a template or a sketch can be made of one half of the design and then be flipped over for tracing the other side. A close duplication can be easily achieved in that way.

To be in balance, an object does not have to be symmetrical. Asymmetrical, or unsymmetrical, shapes are desirable insofar as they, too, remain visually stable. In fact, asymmetry often adds interest through variation. The carving in Figure 2.5 is a case in point. The self-contained asymmetrical carving seems to keep the observer's eye moving throughout, yet a sense of balance and stability exists by virtue of how the carved outline fits within the napkin holder's front panel. The irregularity of the leaf-and-berry design helps avoid monotony that often occurs in the equal distribution of similar shapes.

Figure 2.5. Carved figures, although asymmetric and artistically fluid, appear balanced and stable in an area compatible in shape with the article.

Symmetrical designs tend to lack dynamic appeal. A generalized solution is illustrated in Figure 2.6. It shows graphically how changes in size and shape can radically alter a static design. Be aware that this does not mean static design is wrong. Just as there are excellent still-life paintings, the staidness of statically illustrated decoration has a place in woodcarving.

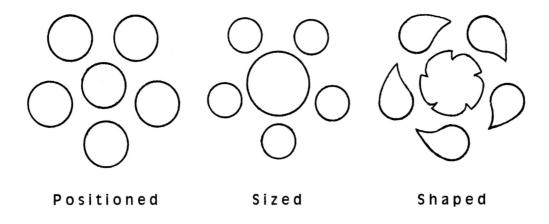

Positioned   Sized   Shaped

Figure 2.6. A static group can be given dynamic qualities by means of sizing and shaping the components.

Another technique to be observed in design pertains to the distribution of separate objects. When designing on paper, visual balance among multiple objects depends essentially on the distribution of areas, while in carving, distribution of mass becomes the challenge. Area and mass are treated much as weights are positioned for support to the sides of a fulcrum in a see-saw. Figure 2.7 compares the two. In effect, the smaller the flower and the lower the weight, the farther either may be placed from a group's balance point.

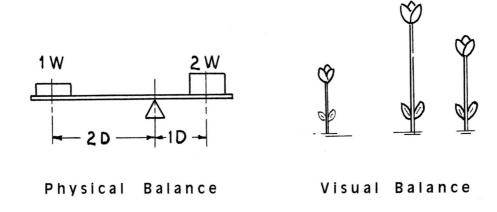

Physical Balance   Visual Balance

Figure 2.7. Visual balance may be obtained by treating areas in drawing (mass in carving) much the same as weight in a balanced see-saw.

Other techniques of importance to the designer are those used to represent depth and distance. Examples of these are illustrated in Figure 2.8. Their use applies mainly to naturalistic carving. Woodcarvings in relief, even in shallow relief, can often be enhanced by their proper application. All procedures seem evident as shown, except for the rendering in perspective. In that application, attention to positioning the line of sight, placing the vanishing points for drawing converging lines, and foreshortening horizontal distances is necessary. The novice might profit by studying the elements of perspective in a series of similar, equally spaced objects, such as a line of telephone poles.

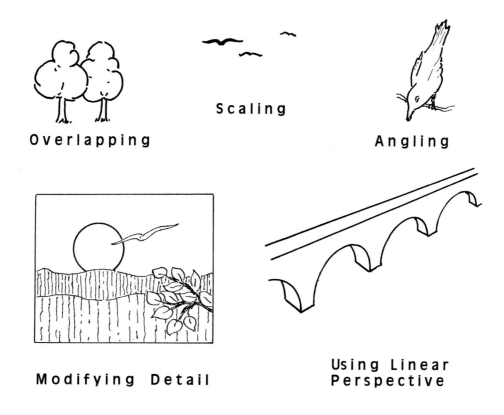

Figure 2.8. The methods of depicting depth and distance in drawing and carving are part of a skillful designer's repertoire.

Construction Procedures

Carving proceeds most expeditiously when coordinated with an article's construction, especially when multiple parts are involved. The ideal time to add a decorative carving occurs when all parts of an item have been prepared to the point of assembly. Individual pieces are likely to be easier to position and tool than are previously assembled objects. This fact generally holds true for large items. Some woods also need to be provided a solid backup. That can be an overriding condition when carving woods hard enough to require the use of a mallet and gouges. Although fully assembled articles may be bought for decorating, they are usually small and made of soft wood that can be easily clamped and carved with little force.

Construction may impose limitations when decorating an article. Both the position and shape of the design are sometimes affected. The decoration may be defined not only by whether incising or relief carving will be appropriate but also whether separate or fully continuous details can be used. Those unfamiliar with this aspect of design might benefit by viewing Figure 2.9. While the incised figures have been symmetrically positioned when viewed from one angle, they are not evenly distributed about the seasoner's circumference. Only three incised figures are used. The seasoner's handle occupies the spot where a fourth equally spaced detail or a continuous design might otherwise have been carved. This application exemplifies how the need to satisfy practical considerations takes precedence over the placement and form of decoration used.

Figure 2.9. Whether used inside or on the patio, a seasoner becomes truly special when enhanced with appropriately executed floral figures.

That type of carving which produces an article, rather than merely decorates it, also subjects design to the practicalities of construction. Design and carving have an integral role in the process. The function intended for each piece essentially defines its design and shaping. A wooden bowl to be made for holding unshelled nuts, for example, will have matters of depth and size largely determined by the quantity of nuts to be held and by what weight and size of bowl can be conveniently passed about when full. The thickness of the wood available constitutes another factor which may impose restrictions on the carved design. Within limitations of this order, design and carving can proceed along any of a variety of paths.

As experienced practitioners know, variations occur within each type of woodcarving. Incised figures may be boldly cut, line cut, chip-carved, edge carved, or a combination of several of these. Relief carvings vary even more. They may be described separately as being plane relief, pierced relief, bas-relief, mid-depth relief, bold relief, and full relief—the latter of which, as previously explained, involves removing all background wood.

Further variation in relief carving may be achieved via the manner of texturing the background. Random gouging is both common and effective, but a form of stippling will often be preferred for small items. The sample board shown in Figure 2.10 indicates the wide range of possibilities. Any one of these textures is likely to be superior to that obtained by efforts to create a smooth, flat background.

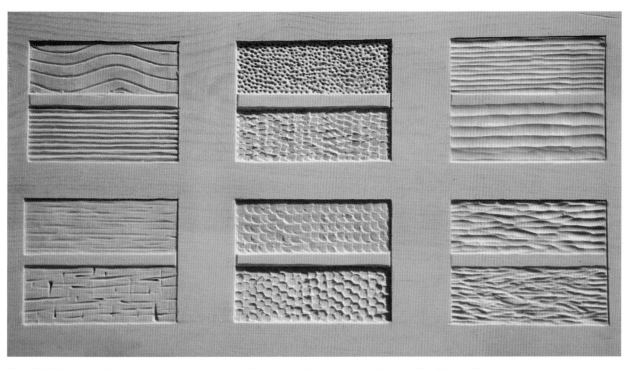

Figure 2.10. Background wood in a relief carving may be V-cut, stippled, or gouged—each of which definitely affects appearance.

Methods which seem to combine elements of incising and relief carving are possible, too. Sectional views of an acorn in three of these less commonly used forms are presented in Figure 2.11. They are: (A) intaglio, a form of inverted relief developed in Greece and widely practiced in Roman times; (B) coelanaglyphic carving, an ancient Egyptian method of forming pictures and figures in shallow relief; and (C) sunken relief, true relief cut below a surface. Discernible differences are apparent in such carvings, even though the top, or surface, view is drawn the same for all.

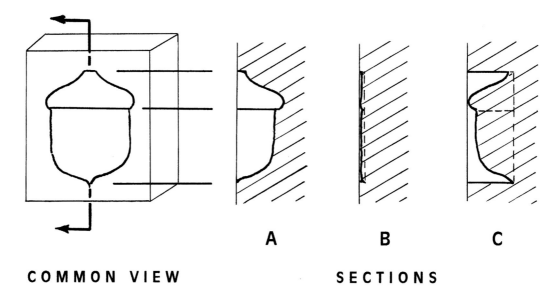

COMMON VIEW   **SECTIONS**

Figure 2.11. Objects in (A) intaglio, (B) coelanaglyphic form, and (C) true sunken relief are cut into the wood and shaped below its surface.

Sources of Design

Inspiration for designs in carving emanates from various sources, including abstract paintings, manufactured items, geometry, and nature. Many designs stem from nature. Representations of plants and animals are particularly common in relief carving, with animal forms dominant among the designs in three-dimensional work. Plant life prevails as the motif of choice for decorating surfaces by relief carving.

The influence of plant life is far reaching. Even in incised carving, where geometric formations are commonly chip carved, one can find examples of floral and leaf-like figures. The sample board shown in Figure 2.12 includes two of them.

Figure 2.12. This board contains examples of some of the many floral and geometric patterns possible by chip carving.

Designs incorporating plant life are frequently modified versions of nature, rather than duplications. Figure 2.13 contains several acceptable modifications. The stylized shapes in these applications are arranged in rhythmically contrived patterns, but they remain true to nature's dictates in areas indicating growth.

Figure 2.13. Designs are often based on plant life, which may be stylized and arranged in rhythmic patterns for borders.

The undulating curve, a form made by repeatedly alternating concave and convex lines, is a powerful tool in design. It may be used effectively for a border, as in the vine-and-leaf arrangement shown, or in shorter segments within a pattern. Illustrations of seaweed offer good possibilities. The plant can be made to appear rhythmically waving in water with its form generally outlined by the two elements of curvature. In practice, the curves are technically designated "cyma recta" and "cyma reversa." Common applications appear in the profiles of certain architectural moldings.

Copying and Creating

When preparing to carve an article, the craftsman may either develop a design or copy one. Beginners are advised to copy designs initially. With the experience that comes with practice and observation, they can then more readily create designs on their own. Copying involves reproducing a given design by any of several methods, including tracing over carbon paper, redrawing using the method of squares, scanning and duplicating via photographic means, or sketching freehand. Sketching requires some practice, but the results possible are worth the effort.

Sketching is a basic tool of the designer. It usually entails using paper and pencil, although experienced persons will sometimes sketch directly on the wood to be carved. Despite this, facsimiles of embellishments are often created beforehand by sketching on paper. An advantage of pencil sketching is the ease with which a design can be created and altered in size, shape, and style. One cannot imagine an artisan being able to create many attractive shapes and decorative forms without first work-

ing out the details freehand. It is a quick and inexpensive way to create alternatives for choosing among.

Many drawings created on paper are transferred to the wood by some means other than sketching. Tracing over carbon paper is a common way to do this, but at times, a cardboard cutout will be evermore helpful. A cardboard template helps assure uniformity of results when outlining elements of a design repeatedly on a surface or when recreating a design on numerous articles. An application is shown in Figure 2.14.

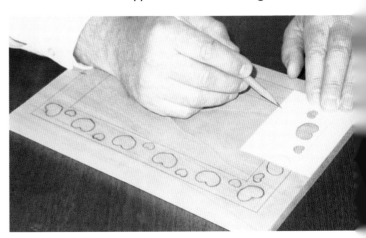

Figure 2.14. Shown in use here is one of several varieties of cardboard templates made for drawing multiple figures uniformly.

An important consideration in this work is artisanship, and its achievement should be a woodcarver's ultimate objective. A matter of creating designs is involved. The craftsman who can duplicate objects closely is undoubtedly a proficient technician, but an ability also to do the design work places the individual in a higher category of achievement. Persons who make lifelike carvings of animals in one position or another are essentially copiers. They deserve little if any credit for the designs, no matter how skillfully and realistically shaped the figures may be. The subjects already exist in every detail in nature. Thus, an ability to create and carve designs effectively distinguishes the artisan from the technician whose skill is limited to carving.

Stylizing is a way of designing. The process involves interpretation. Even if a finished piece represents something real, the act of forming it in a style other than that observed involves creative effort. Something similar can be said of nonrepresentational pieces.

When learning, the procedure recommended for many is, first, to reproduce patterns and figures as given and, second, to begin modifying them by altering their internal features and outlined shapes. Persons sufficiently skilled in doing those things can then more readily move on to designing. Attention to matters of artistic expression grows in importance with each stage in this process of learning. The more one works without previously completed models to follow, the more that person must rely on established principles of esthetics. Subsequent sections and chapters contain relevant applications of those principles. They will be helpful in developing a "feel" for practices which have become second nature to accomplished artists and product designers.

Chapter Three
Decorating Desk Accessories

A writing desk in the home can be an efficient work station. It can also be a place to contemplate things of beauty when relaxing between tasks. The designer, therefore, necessarily concentrates on making the place attractive without affecting utility. Achieving harmony in the construction and decoration of the accessories becomes a major part of the challenge.

Functional Choices

Useful articles of several kinds will often be kept at a desk. Among these are devices for containing or holding pens, pencils, books, paper clips, letters, and stacks of paper. Other items sometimes made of wood for use at the work station include a letter knife, a paperweight, and a "secretary," the latter for holding several items at once. The articles, if individually made, can be adorned with hand-carved designs to impart to each a special uniqueness.

In the material presented hereafter, the applications are intended to foster a sense of decorative design. Ample opportunities for individual creativity are present. Although the items may be embellished precisely as shown, the designs may be altered and interchanged or be replaced entirely with patterns of one's preference. A design-conscious carver might also give thought to the purpose in carrying a motif consistently throughout an entire set of accessories. Whatever the choice, the need to observe the principles of design and utility remains prevalent.

Bookrack Decorations

A means of keeping a dictionary, a reference or two, and a few other selections within arms reach when at the desk is virtually essential. A small, substantially constructed wooden bookrack may do. One made about 5 1/2 inches wide, with 6-inch tall uprights and a distance of about 12 inches between the uprights, will ordinarily suffice. A larger assembly could be cumbersome when filled with books. The dimensions given will be useful for anyone desiring to make and decorate a bookrack.

As to appearance, a bookrack's vertical parts provide for many options. Their tops may be rounded, tapered, squared, or be given some combination of these shapes. The shape used helps define the outline of the area to be decorated. There are few other restrictions. The design may be carved in relief or by incising, and the motif chosen may fall within a range that varies from the realistic to the abstract.

The design in Figure 3.1 is one of the many geometric patterns applicable to a bookrack. It illustrates several important points about chip carving. For one thing, an overall pattern of repetitive type, formerly referred to as "diaper work," may seem very monotonous. The key to counteracting this possible effect is to incise a different form within the broad array of cells. The spot selected must not upset the pattern's visual balance, but the shape to carve there remains very much open to individual discretion. The design shown contains a fitting solution.

While the entire pattern may be worked out on paper initially, the final layout for chip carving is best drawn directly on the wood using instruments. Items used for sizing cells and drawing straight lines on the bookrack are shown in Figure 3.2. If the pattern had contained many curved features, a mechanical aid for drawing arcs and circles would be an additional need.

Figure 3.1. Monotony in repetitive chip-carved patterns can be avoided by strategically locating a different shape, as in this bookrack's decoration.

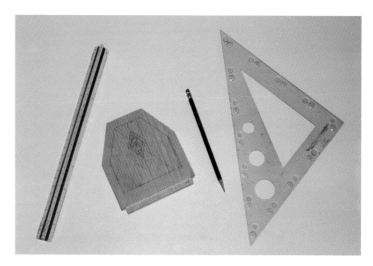

Figure 3.2. Drawing instruments help provide the precision needed in a layout for carving a geometric pattern.

After carving a bookrack, a decision must be made about whether or not to apply an oil stain. This is essentially a matter of personal choice. Stain has a marked effect on a pattern cut into light wood, such as pine. As in the chip-carved bookrack, stain darkens the deep corners of the incised cells. Wiping the wet stain with a dry cloth highlights some parts while imparting prominence to the design overall. The color does not have to be very dark to be effective, but before staining and applying a sealing finish of any kind, it is important to erase all pencil lines that have not been removed by carving.

A second bookrack, one made of spruce and decorated with a naturalistic scene, is pictured in Figure 3.3. Except for the carving and the wood used, its details basically duplicate those given for the previous example. The manner in which the water weeds well from the border and remain in the same plane produces an unusual effect. This technique gives the design an appearance of being an integral part of the wood.

Timing is important in the drawing and carving of an article comprised of several pieces. Figures 3.4 and 3.5 illustrate this point. Sketching the layout and gouging the details proceed best after the shaping and sanding operations have been completed and the parts of the article are still unassembled.

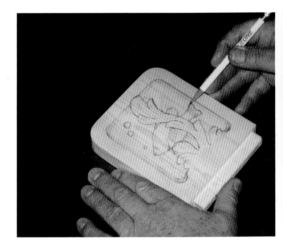

Figure 3.4. An experienced woodcarver will often sketch the final layout directly onto the part to be carved.

Figure 3.5. Drawing and carving proceed best on bookracks and many other multiple-piece projects before the parts are assembled.

Figure 3.3. The flat water weeds effectively tie this naturalistic scene in relief to the project's border.

Technique is important, also. An experienced woodcarver will often prefer to draw a scene freehand rather than trace it onto the part to be carved. Nevertheless, sketching first on paper to work out the details remains a strong recommendation. The technique to observe when carving is to avoid undercutting parts of the design. This can be accomplished by slightly slanting the blade from the vertical when making stop and outline cuts about the perimeter and edges of the figures.

For carving small parts in a wood of soft texture, a bench hook will be most useful if one strip has been notched like that in Figure 3.5. Firm woods, on the other hand, are best carved with a jig made for holding pieces while driving gouges with a mallet. Figures 3.6 and 3.7 illustrate the use of a jig of suitable form for carving flat pieces of cherry wood. Such things must be considered when designing, for knowledge of the skills and equipment required and available must be present in order to create a design that can be completed as intended. A similar recommendation applies relative to power carving.

Figure 3.6. A mallet and jig are practically essential when gouging wood as hard and firm as cherry.

Figure 3.7. Power carving is most helpful for shaping and cutting wood to a uniform depth in tight spots.

The closely spaced flowers and petals in the decoration leave only enough room for power carving and stippling the background. A tool for stippling can be made by grinding the point of a nail to the shape desired. It is then repeatedly tapped across the background wood that has been routed to depth. This process obliterates any unevenness created by power carving. A pattern of stippling can be carried close to the raised details, thereby avoiding the fuzziness which sometimes results when gouging the background along edges. Figure 3.8 displays the assembly with its stylized design.

Figure 3.9. A gift based on knowledge of the recipient's interests adds an element of significance to the design.

Figure 3.8. A floral design (this one with a stippled background) can be readily adapted to a project's shape.

Further illustration of the techniques of decorative design may be observed in the catalpa-wood bookrack in Figure 3.9. The design is simple, having been styled for a particular person, a clergyman. Simplicity and relevance of design provide the strength. Notice in this application, as well as in several others done in relief, how a narrowly gouged line surrounds the raised details. This practice cleans up the ends of gouged marks where they come against adjacent forms, and it appears to increase the depth of tooling throughout. Be aware that catalpa wood is soft and tends to chip when tooled. Thus, it cannot be easily decorated with small or intricate details. It is entirely appropriate for designs having comparatively large details, and the wood's beautiful grain makes it especially desirable for the applications of the kind shown.

Paper-Knife Design

The paper knife, a tool used for cutting folded sheets and opening sealed letters, makes an appropriate companion-piece at a desk. It is another item whose structure lends itself to different styles and methods of decoration. Incised and relief carving are basic possibilities. These may be applied in almost any of their various forms.

The first requirement to be satisfied for constructing a wooden paper knife is to select a species that can be worked readily yet will hold detail firmly. Cherry wood has excellent qualities for the purpose. It responds nicely to carving tools, and its surface will not wear away rapidly. With ordinary use, a paper knife of good wood will maintain the necessary sharpness of cutting edge and firmness of decorative detail for years. An important point to be observed in the shaping of a knife's blade is to make the edge sharp and sufficiently pointed for ease in opening sealed envelopes.

Although paper knives can be made and assembled from two pieces, there seems to be little reason for doing so. One-piece construction does not require a joint for attaching parts, and there is no need to be concerned about a joint's strength. A single piece 8 or 9 inches long and a little more than an inch across will usually be adequate. A knife of solid, durable construction, having been fashioned from a board of cherry heartwood, is shown in Figure 3.10.

Figure 3.10. The paper knife in cherry wood illustrated here is an application of carving in the round to a useful product.

The three-dimensional carving of the stylized owl decorating the handle of the knife represents one of many possibilities. Of importance is the assistance in gripping provided by the figure's configuration. Equally important, particularly from the standpoint of product design, is the creation of a sharp, pointed blade. An abrading cylinder (Figure 3.11) and drum sanders in a drill press are useful for obtaining the shape desired.

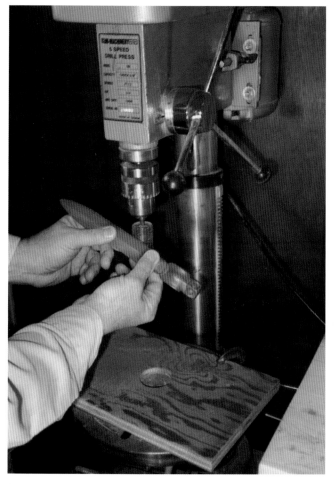

Figure 3.11. Whether shaped by whittling or abrading, as here, a sharp, pointed blade is as important as using durable wood in a letter opener.

With a little thought, a carver can create and substitute features of his or her liking. A handle's embellishment can be easily arranged to suit some personal interest, but a concern to be remembered when doing that is to avoid sharp protrusions. Properly done, a handle will assist when gripping without producing an uncomfortable feeling. The design in Figure 3.12 shows the fish's fins subdued for this very reason.

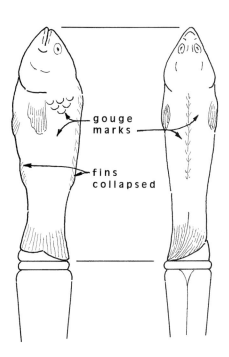

gouge marks

fins collapsed

Figure 3.12. The handle of a paper knife can sometimes be fashioned to suggest one's hobby or special interest.

A paper knife made by carving a hardwood branch in geometric style is shown in Figure 3.13. The diamonds are the result of incising crisscross outlines and embellishing the cells with acrylic paint. While color adds to the article's attractiveness, the tooling alone on the handle's surface, though shallow, adds to the piece's utilitarian value. Coats of satin polyurethane on both the painted and unpainted portions protect the knife's surface.

Figure 3.13. A pattern of lines incised on an object's handle not only produces a decorative effect but also aids in holding and gripping.

When creating a diamond pattern, the layout of the grid may very well be the most difficult part of the process to accomplish. Figure 3.14 gives helpful tips. Work out the pattern on paper first, then transfer it to the round handle. Complete a layout on paper by (1) drawing a rectangle with lines spaced equal to the wood's circumference and pattern height, as shown, (2) dividing this rectangle with horizontal and vertical lines according to the size and number of cells wanted, and (3) drawing lines on an angle through intersecting points of the grid. Several drawings on paper may be needed initially in order to determine the cell size and number most effective for the article's handle. All lines may be sketched, because a final, more exact layout will be needed only on the wood.

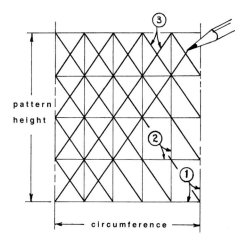

pattern height

circumference

Figure 3.14. A grid for drawing diamonds of appropriate size and number should be finalized on paper before constructing lines on the wood.

Drawing the pattern on the wood can be accomplished by marking distances and penciling lines freehand to form the grid. A strip of paper marked with measurements provides a good means of laying off circumferential distances. Parts of the grid needed, as shown in Figure 3.15, include points of intersection for drawing the angled lines, which can be sketched neatly by following an edge of tape spiraled through the intersections. When completed, the diamonds are formed by incising 3/32 of an inch deep V-grooves where the angled lines fall. The carving of these spiral grooves on the round stock can be readily achieved with the flat blade of a whittling knife. Painting and sealing finish the item.

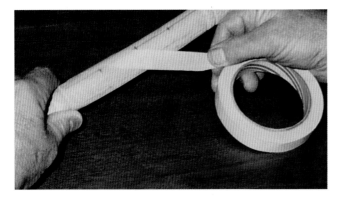

Figure 3.15. Masking tape wrapped along points of intersection assists when drawing angled lines to guide the grooving of the diamond pattern.

When creating designs for paper knives, thought must be devoted to the appropriateness of the decoration. Some designs are more suitable than others when carving articles cut from branches or saplings. One in particular, the rope pattern, fits especially well. In fact, it is most easily carved along a round shaft. A round handle so carved makes an effective handgrip. Something made similar to that represented in Figure 3.16 will produce the result desired.

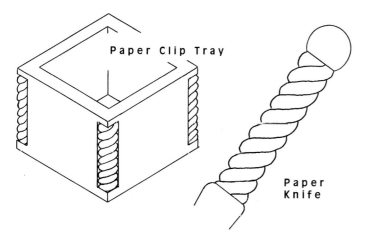

Figure 3.16. Rope patterns are more easily and suitably carved along sharp edges and round handles than on flat surfaces.

Paper and Fastener Dispensers

With a little more difficulty, a rope pattern may be carved along a container's sharp exterior edges. The small tray in the accompanying drawing provides an example. However, some locations are to be avoided completely. Flat surfaces where the design would be shaped to no more than half the rope's normal thickness are among them. Difficulty in carving, because of limited roundness and depth, is the main reason.

With a tray for holding paper clips at hand, there must be paper available. Some provision for writing at the desk is essential, anyway. Paper for jotting down notes, penciling messages, and drawing sketches is a highly useful addition. Letter-size sheets can be cut in half and assembled in a stack 5 1/2 inches wide x 8 1/2 inches long for those purposes. Scrap paper, clear on one side, may be adequate.

The objective in this application is to keep the sheets handy and in good order. A tray made like that shown in Figure 3.17 will provide the convenience desired. Its construction consists of 5/16-inch pine sized and assembled for containing a pack of paper of the dimensions recommended above. The need to provide some clearance around the stack of paper seems obvious. Providing an open end in the unit also allows for easy insertion and removal of the note paper.

Figure 3.17. The colorful abstraction embellishing the top piece of this paper dispenser was inspired by autumn leaves.

As generally holds true in this work, the style of decoration to be used remains optional. The type of carving remains open to personal choice, too. An abstractly incised configuration decorates the paper dispenser shown. Although its inspiration has been drawn from autumn leaves, the colorful areas among the gouged lines are only slightly representational. For the most part, the artistic merit of the design rests on considerations of balance, coherence, and diversity. The visual interest created may very well be the decoration's strongest point.

Letter Holders

A handy accessory in any household is one constructed for holding letters received or placed there for mailing. It may be decorated with an incised design or be carved in relief in the conventionalized form applied to the holder pictured in Figure 3.18. The design has the formalized features of a symmetrical arrangement. Although stylized, it remains representational. Its orientation to nature seems obvious.

Figure 3.18. Harmony between the conventionalized carving and the maple letter holder is achieved by congruency of form in an important area.

Made of maple, the holder has a 5/8-inch thick base and uprights of 7/16-inch thickness. It has a 3-inch overall depth at the uprights, a 5-inch width, and a 5 1/2-inch height, with the carved member about 3/4 of an inch shorter than the one to the rear. The assembly accommodates letters of ordinary size.

The design's outline and the top edge of the front panel of the item provide a measure of compatibility. The curvatures are elliptical. Some other confining shape could be used as long as the two points remain in visual harmony, but then both the floral design and its gouged background might also have to be changed. In any case, the maple wood has a firmness that will hold finely carved details well.

Form based on nature can be appealing, whether made completely realistic in appearance or altered in some way. Figure 3.19 contains an incised design that seems somewhat more natural than the one previously shown. Its lifelike elements are displayed in balanced distribution without the use of symmetry. The arrangement creates a considerable degree of interest as a consequence of our familiarity with naturally grown, windblown plants. It is another example of how asymmetric form can be represented in a naturalistic style.

Chip-carved patterns also make interesting decorations on letter holders. Figure 3.20 displays one such application that could be easily duplicated or modified. The wood is pine. Simplicity of design and the use of a different shape in the center of the carving establish much of the application's effectiveness.

Notice the placement of the pattern a short distance above the surface's true center. Something similar may be seen in other items having a vertical surface. The efficacy of doing this follows the reasoning given in Chapter 2 for placing carved patterns optically, rather than by physical measurement.

Figure 3.19. Although incised, the decoration on this cherry-wood letter holder remains distinctly naturalistic.

Figure 3.20. This simple chip-carved pattern is evidence that a decoration need not be elaborate to be effective.

The Desk Secretary

The pine container shown in Figure 3.21 holds a pen, pencil, and paper notes outside and postage stamps, erasers, a glue stick, a paper punch, and a stapler inside. Its 3 1/2 x 7 1/2 x 8 1/2-inch overall size could probably accommodate still more useful items. Considering all that the container can keep handily available, one can readily understand how it came to be called a "secretary."

Figure 3.21. A desk secretary, while useful in many ways, becomes even more desirable when decorated in bold relief.

The accessory is as appealing as it is useful. The boldly carved decoration makes it exceptional. The leaf-and-berry arrangement has a carved depth of about half the thickness of the 9/16-inch board used. Contrived in form, the details fit neatly within bounds of the 3 1/2 x 6-inch surface, with a 3/4-inch border surrounding the decoration. The optical and measured centers are the same in this application. The lid's nearly horizontal position is the reason.

The secretary would make a worthwhile and beautiful addition on almost any desk, particularly if included among other accessories decorated with carvings of similar design. A design having a motif much like the one on the secretary decorates an article presented in the previous chapter. It is evidence that the design on the secretary could be carved on articles made of comparatively thin material, though not as deep.

Chapter 4
Enhancing Boxes,
Cabinets, and Chests

Wooden boxes, cabinets, and chests, large and small, serve beneficial purposes in the home. The uses are extensive. Jewelry, pins, needles, buttons, pencils, kitchen utensils, blankets, garments, and practically anything else that must be stored in a readily available place are often kept in the wooden containers. While the functions may vary from item to item, the fundamental purpose of carving each is simply to decorate one or more exterior surfaces. Only occasionally will something, such as a name or trademark, be carved inside an item to denote ownership.

The Options

Anyone planning to carve a box or chest must make several important decisions. First, there must be a determination as to whether or not a carved design will be appropriate. The wood to be used may be decorative enough without it. One should probably not add a carving, for example, to a small knickknack box constructed of birds-eye or curly maple. The same thinking applies regarding the use of burl or a figurative crotch wood. Little would be gained by cutting into wood having beautifully figured grain in order to replace it with a carved design, to say nothing of the difficulty in tooling likely to be encountered.

Second, a decision must be made concerning the style and placement of a carving on an item to be decorated. Some pieces of furniture done in the style of an earlier period of time often have carved legs and handles. Frequently, the carvings are decorative additions to form leaf-like hand grips, abstractly figured projections on cabriole legs, and ball-and-claw configurations on the feet, most of which are anachronistic on chests of modern design. In short, period styles are most fitting on items done in the styles of bygone periods.

As to location, the front panel of large chests provides a good surface for carving. The top and front surfaces are the most used spots on small boxes and chests. None should be overdecorated, whatever the application.

The third decision has to do with form. The method of carving and a design's general features come into view at this point. For the most part, simultaneous determinations are involved. The design's form depends on whether the details are incised or carved in relief, just as the method of carving depends on the form given the design. These determinations precede the preparation of the specific details of the design.

The fourth, and final, decision to be addressed here involves structuring the design. How its shape will be made to fit the area to decorated, whether it will be representative of something or be a nonrepresentative abstraction, and the extent to which the final configuration will be appropriate for the application are matters to be drawn to conclusion. Occasionally, a design can be made to relate in some way to the proposed contents of the item being decorated. The result is a definite plus when that can be done. Several of the designs in this chapter indicate such a relationship, but others serve their purpose adequately without relating to anything the container holds.

Decorating Boxes

Boxes intended for setting on desks, bureaus, or shelves are often made cylindrical in shape or are given the 90-degree corners of rectangular forms. Involved are considerations of utility and convenience in construction. The shapes are basic, but the sizes and uses vary. Jewelry, writing accessories, and odds and ends of all sorts are commonly kept in the small, transportable containers.

Small boxes generally do not need much embellishment. A neatly carved design on the top, or lid, will usually suffice. The side areas are ordinarily too confined. Many already contain some detail where the lid meets the body.

After determining which surface to decorate, the next step involves drawing a layout that will fit appropriately while creating a sense of variety. The chip-carved application shown in Figure 4.1 serves as an example. Although centered for balance, the series of arcs along the outer edge of the pattern conform to the circular surface in a general way. That feature adds variety without upsetting the symmetry involved. The circular elements within the pattern harmonize effectively with the item's shape, while virtually compelling the viewer to study the several interesting shapes created within the pattern. Elements of order, diversity, and balance are inherent in the decoration.

Figure 4.1. Well-designed chip-carved patterns on round surfaces satisfy visual requirements of order, balance, coherence, compatibility, and variety.

Figure 4.2. A sharply pointed knife and a notched bench hook are particularly useful for removing curved chips from small cylindrical pieces.

The woodcarver who has never before chip carved a curved pattern will find that some tools work better than others. A flat blade with a pointed tip is most productive. One is pictured in use in Figure 4.2. The shape allows for ease in cutting sharp curves, whereas a wider blade will not define the form as readily. Notice, also, how a notched strip on the bench hook assists when carving a circular piece.

The design on the cylindrical box has no definite relationship to its contents, but that on the rectangular box presented in Figure 4.3 is intended to do so. The pine box, 11 inches long by 4 inches wide and 3 1/2 inches high, is made for holding pencils, and the airy, thinly incised lines on its lid are script-like representations. Any similarity to calligraphic writing is deliberate. Although the association might not be immediately apparent in this case, an effort to create a decoration that conforms to or indicates the article's contents is a worthwhile undertaking.

Figure 4.3. This rhythmical tracery of incised lines, as punctuated with incised chips, adds considerable interest to the pencil box.

Other relationships might be more evident. Consider this for decorating a box of some kind: (1) an emblem of a military branch or veteran's organization on a wooden container for holding a former serviceman's memorabilia, (2) a dog of appropriate breed portrayed on the lid of a box containing a pet's registration papers and grooming equipment, (3) a religious symbol or scene on the wooden case protecting the family Bible, (4) a colorful pallet and brushes on a receptacle for artist's paints, and (5) a fish on a container of lures and artificial bait. An imaginative woodcarver needs only a little creative inspiration to produce other acceptable themes. The possibilities are considerable.

Lacking a desirable relationship between a design for a box and its contents, the interests of the person who will own or use the box could give a clue to its decoration. This, too, involves a principle to be observed. While a floral design might suit a certain housewife, and a whitetail deer in relief might interest a hunter, an error of gross proportions could be perpetrated by giving either person a gift that has been decorated without regard to those individual preferences.

Line and Outline Carving

The form of carving used to create the undulating decorative pattern on the rectangular box is line carving. The method will sometimes be referred to as "outline carving" if the lines define an object's shape. Either way, it is a specialized method of incising. The method is similar to chip carving by virtue of flat-sided tools being used exclusively. Whereas chip carving mainly involves removing triangular, pyramidal, or curvilinear chips using knives and, perhaps, a skew chisel, line carving involves the removal of thin strips of V-shaped wood with knives and, possibly, a V-tool. Skill in using the tools must be present in both cases.

Not all line-carved patterns are given border lines that conform to the woods' outline. As is apparent in the illustration of the pencil box, there are no straight lines to confine the carved decoration or to duplicate the lid's shape. The decoration follows the rectangular outline of the lid only in a general way. Notice, however, the relatively broad areas of uncarved wood left in place about the symmetrical pattern. These help keep the viewer's eye within the limits of the article. Areas of plain wood made too narrow about the perimeter would tend to have the pointed carving direct the eye beyond the ends of the lid.

Because artistic applications of line carving are comparatively rare today, a brief explanation of the process seems in order. The procedure is simply a matter of drawing lines on the wood, such as in Figure 4.4, and replacing them with narrow V-shaped channels. After drawing the design where desired on the wood's surface, continuous vertical incisions are made with sharp knife and steady hand throughout the full length of each line. Grooving then begins by cutting beside each line with the knife's blade angled at about 30 degrees from a vertical plane. The object of this cut is to remove one half of the channel's final shape. The third cut, again alternating direction as necessary to cut properly in relation to the grain, is to incise along the opposite side of the centerline. This cut can be made as stated for the previous step. It may also be done with the side of a V-tool. In fact, a 60 degree V-tool may be preferred. It will fit against the side already incised and, thereby, provide support for maintaining uniformity of width along the finished line.

Figure 4.4. Border, corner, and central designs may be line carved on surfaces of many shapes.

Figure 4.5. A line for a border can often be most easily drawn by guiding the pencil while a finger follows the edge.

Figure 4.6. A flat blade may be used for carving the V-grooves of straight and moderately curved lines.

Figure 4.7. A tool shaped like that shown is superior to others with flat blades when carving sharply curved outlines.

The use of a flat blade for some of the incising avoids the tearing of wood against the grain sometimes encountered along a side when attempting to incise a groove in one cut with a V-tool. This problem may occur when cutting across the wood's grain, because one side of the V-tool will be going against the grain. If such tearing is likely to occur, a flat blade should be used in its place to cut in the proper direction along one side of a groove. Equally important as the need for a clean cut is the need for uniformity in the finished groove. The accompanying photographs illustrate some of the important techniques.

Wall Boxes

A type of box of considerable use, though not a common fixture in homes today, is the wall box. A small one will serve handily for holding notes, flyers, letters, and pencils. Its value might be most appreciated in a modern home if placed beside the telephone.

In colonial America, boxes were mounted on walls in various locations and for different purposes. Those kept near a place of rest or relaxation sometimes held tobacco, pipes, and snuff, while those in the kitchen were customarily used for holding candles, salt, spoons, forks, and knives. Some were provided with lids; some had drawers. Their utility was evident.

A wall box of contemporary use is shown in Figure 4.8. A similar piece can be easily constructed using 1/2-inch pine. Parts are assembled with butt joints, a good grade of glue, and brads where end grain meets the side pieces. The sizes may be varied to suit, but a 7-inch width and 4 1/2-inch depth of pocket are suggested.

Figure 4.8. A single flower, even when created by chip carving, can be placed so that the wood's grain and untouched area provide artistic balance.

The decoration on the box's front stands in distinct contrast to that on the pencil box presented earlier. Both designs are incised, but the portrayal of a flower in uniquely incised chip-carved form has little relationship to the rhythmically undulating lines of the other. Moreover, one is symmetrically balanced, and the other is informally arranged. In both applications, areas of bare wood effectively offset the decorations.

The possibilities of decorating by incising go well beyond the designs on these two items. Not only are combinations of line and chip carving possible, as shown to a limited extent in the pencil box, but also incising by gouging can be combined with line carving with interesting results. Applications worthy of the challenge are shown in Figure 4.9. All three are reproductions of patterns once gouged and line carved into panels of doors on early American cupboards and cabinets. What they represent seems apparent, despite their contrived features.

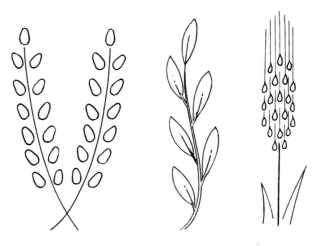

Figure 4.9. Gouged and line-incised images found in early folk-art applications on cabinet doors and sideboards are still applicable today.

Whether incising or working in relief, the carving must be preceded by an accurate layout, especially if uniformly sized, shaped, and spaced elements are part of the design. Precision may then be essential. As illustrated in previous chapters, drawing instruments of several kinds and templates are very useful at such times.

Cabinets

Decorations on cabinets are usually most visible if placed on a front surface. The front is often a door. The piece to receive the decoration must be made ready for assembly but be left unattached for the drawing and carving operations. The process has advanced to the point of carving in Figure 4.10.

Figure 4.10. Soft pine of homogeneous grain can be deeply gouged without the use of a mallet.

When drawing directly or tracing a design onto wood, the instrument must not be pressed so hard that it will leave deep grooves. Relief carving will remove lightly sketched lines and shallow indentations, but deeply grooved marks can be difficult to eradicate. This concern may be most pertinent when carving in low relief. Only very light sanding, if any at all, can be tolerated before applying the finish. Light penciling, such as that outside the area being carved in the accompanying illustration, can later be removed without ill effect.

The floral design on the wall cabinet emanates from the bottom of the carved area (Figure 4.11). This form of decoration is most properly applied to parts mounted in a vertical position, thereby, simulating natural growth. The areas surrounding the flower also have a significant role in the design. The vertical, randomly gouged background makes the smooth floral parts stand out prominently, and the pattern's outline fits the door of the 5 x 11 x 16-inch cabinet with a welcome departure from a straight-lined rectangular shape.

Figure 4.11. Figures carved in relief, including those symmetrically arranged, have a realistic quality not achieved by other methods.

Figure 4.12. Carved leaves and flowers that appear to stem from a root source simulate realistic growth.

Another floral pattern suitable for vertical positioning may be observed in Figure 4.12. Although the components are somewhat contrived, they appear in naturalistic form due partly to the stems emerging from a root source. The design as drawn is intended for carving a rectangular surface. Because most doors are rectangular, the design could be effective on the front of cabinets of many different sizes. Proportionality, as well as sizing, becomes a concern of considerable importance when adapting a design like that to an area of different rectangularity.

A drawing of this type may be altered to fit other shapes, too. There are several useful hints to observe when doing so. These include the previously observed practice of having the general outline of the drawing follow the edges of the surface to be decorated, making some parts of the floral object point somewhat toward the corners, and adding more flowers or leaves if they seem to fit in naturally without creating clutter. For the sake of esthetics, the rhythmic curvature of stems should be maintained while avoiding unsightly distortions of the naturalistic components.

Utensil and Blanket Chests

Whatever the article to be embellished may be, relief carving can add a sense of realism by virtue of contour and depth. It produces a quality not seen in the flatness of line carving or in the sharpness of chip carving. Much of the desirable effect is due to our familiarity with the roundness and flowing quality of three-dimensional natural form and the fact that perfect straightness cannot be readily observed except in man-made work. Items carved in relief often have an unequaled richness as a consequence. Considering what this method of carving can add to a wooden piece, it should be given serious consideration when planning to decorate articles of notable value.

Consider the 3 x 9 x 11-inch chest shown in Figure 4.13. It holds a full set of silverware. The relationship of the carving on the chest to the utensils bears special consideration. The pattern carved between the parallel grooves on the top surface, though not a duplication, is vaguely similar to that decorating the handles of the knives, forks, and spoons kept inside. The designs on the handles are nothing more than the source of inspiration for the plant-like abstraction on the cover.

The decoration does not follow ordinary methods of styling, particularly in relation to placement and form. The carving's restriction within lines made straight by guiding a gouge along a straight edge, its confinement to a relatively small area of the surface, and its position off-center for best effect are not the most ordinary practices. The concave sloping of the background to create depth and contrast is another special feature of the design.

Figure 4.13. The impressive relief carving on this chest captures the essence of the abstract design on the utensils kept inside.

As with relief carvings generally, the background was gouged in the direction of the wood's grain. The artistic qualities of the small carving definitely negated the need for more elaborate tooling or the application of stain for contrast. Several coats of a clear, satin finish proved to be entirely sufficient.

Carvings in strip form are sometimes used to decorate a surface in the manner of a border. Unlike many individual embellishments in strip form, borders are usually continuous and symmetrically arranged. They, as with individual strips, are frequently used where much of the wood's surface is to remain plain and in view.

The tracing of a border may be seen in Figure 4.14. Relief carving in one of its several forms would probably be most suitable for a nonrepresentational design of this kind. Shallow relief and plane relief are recommended, although outline carving offers another possibility. The stippling of background wood seems appropriate for the applications in relief.

Figure 4.14. Decorative carvings in the form of borders or individual strips are sometimes more effective than those covering broad areas.

Large objects are often carved in a form other than a simple border or isolated strip. Chests made for setting on the floor are among them. Their size, alone, makes them eligible for patterns covering large areas. Any woodcarver interested in carving something of significant worth should consider applying his or her skill to a blanket chest.

Chests have long been part of American tradition. Immigrants to this country often brought their possessions from Europe in large wooden chests, and throughout the years, American households have consistently kept one or more of the wooden containers about for storing personal belongings. Blankets, sheets, clothing, and other foldable materials have been packed into the structures—some of which were plain while others were painted or specially decorated by carving. The solidly constructed and uniquely embellished chests of the Pennsylvania Germans have become particularly highly prized by collectors.

Whatever the decorative treatment given a chest, in early times an individually crafted piece was usually given as part of a dowry for a particular young lady whose name may have been emblazoned on the underside of the chest's lid. No wonder that the sentimentality attached has led such items to be passed from generation to generation as priceless heirlooms. Perhaps the one in Figure 4.15 has such potential.

Figure 4.15. A personally designed and carved blanket chest is an excellent means of passing evidence of one's talent on to following generations.

Made years ago in high school, the piece shown continues to endure the wear of time. The overall size of the sturdy chest, 36 inches long by 20 inches wide and 21 inches high, assures its functionality. It holds items as intended, and its smooth lid at the height indicated enables one to be seated comfortably for short periods. The wood exhibits the reddish color so characteristic of aged pine, and the individually created relief carving adds a markedly distinctive touch. The balanced, rhythmic, and subtly varied arrangement and treatment of details deserve close scrutiny. Had the design been created by a more experienced person, a more varied shaping of the leaves might have occurred. Nevertheless, the work in its present form has many positive features and artistic qualities to commend it.

Originality is but one factor to the young craftsman's credit. The carving along the bottom member of the chest is different, too. The undulating shapes there are achieved by a form of edge carving—a process described in detail in a later chapter.

Chapter Five
Creating Unique Coin Banks

Wooden containers for storing hard currency need not be plain or unattractive. They may be given a special "look." Proficiently carved features make a difference.

There are two basic forms of wooden coin banks, each providing the craftsman with ample opportunities to apply individual artistic and technical skills. Some of the containers are geometric assemblies of flat boards that contain a limited amount of carved work, and others are tooled completely about their outer surface to create a three-dimensional figure of some kind. Both types are presented in detail in this chapter. By following the material given, a diligent person can build upon the special aspects of design and carving involved and soon be creating unique products of his or her own design.

Basic Forms

One form of geometrically shaped bank is boxlike. Its rectilinear form simplifies construction and carving, being readily decorated by incising, by relief carving, or by attaching a carved applique to a flat surface. This type of structure can be embellished much in the manner of square-cornered boxes, except that on banks the decorations are generally restricted to the front panel. A bank's top contains a slot for receiving coins, and the side panels are not ordinarily within the central point of viewing.

Another geometric type of bank is cylindrical. Construction begins by laminating pieces of wood for turning on a lathe. As with all coin banks, the center must be hollow to receive the coins. For the sake of appearance, this type of bank will sometimes be painted after carving in order to hide the glue lines created by building up pieces to the thickness desired.

Banks of another form, those shaped by carving, may be decorated with a representational shape. A piggy bank of wood exemplifies the type. Its construction follows the procedure recommended for all wooden banks, with the external carving occurring after the shaping of other parts. The steps for doing the decorating are similar to those proposed for carving solid items in the round. Unlike carved figures that have no utilitarian value, however, one made for holding coins must have an internal cavity. Therein lies the special challenge. Besides representing a creature or other body, provisions for inserting coins, holding them, and periodically removing some are essential.

Box Banks

Figure 5.1 presents an example of an easily made box bank. All joints are butt joints. A good grade of carpenter's glue holds the squared pieces of catalpa wood securely together without the aid of more intricate joinery.

The carving of this piece is also relatively easy to do. The catalpa needs no more embellishment than the carved strip and the coves routed along the top and bottom edges. The wood's grain offsets the narrow details nicely. Done in relief, the alternated flowers and leaves are carved about 3/16 of an inch deep. Small, rotary, power-driven burrs prove useful for shaping the background in designs like this that are too confined for hand tooling.

Figure 5.1. The narrow strip in relief on the front of this coin bank indicates once again that a design need not be elaborate to be attractive.

Basic requirements are satisfied by making box banks about 4 3/4 inches wide, 7 1/2 inches high, and 3 3/4 inches deep, overall. These dimensions may be increased or decreased somewhat, but the craftsman should keep in mind that a rectangle outlining the front surface is considered to be most pleasing in the proportions of the "golden rectangle," a shape sized approximately 5 units by 8 units. With the wood planed to 9/16-inch thickness, the cavity resulting from the assembly provides enough space for coins in substantial number.

For receiving coins, a slot cut 3/16-inch wide, about 1 1/2 inches long, and on center in the top member is adequate. This can be made by drilling and sawing. A small file may be useful, as well.

Any of several useful devices can be built into the base for removing coins from a wooden bank. One device is nothing more than a square or rectangular piece of plastic recessed into the bottom, being fastened there with small round-head screws at its corners. This simple arrangement allows for viewing the contents, and it provides a bit of security, in that, coins are not as easily removed as can be done with a freely sliding mechanism.

Figure 5.2 provides a view of a built-in slide for retaining and removing coins. The mechanism's convenience seems obvious. It does require a bit more work in construction than the fixed variety, but the extra effort required for housing the slide will often produce preferable results. If desired, a single screw can be inserted through or alongside the slide when closed to keep it from being opened too easily. This feature might be desired by families with small children.

The manner of decorating box banks has practically no limit. Shapes drawn for incising the front panel are acceptable (Figure 5.3), as are designs for strips of chip carving. Patterns suitable for relief carving panels range widely in size from ribbon-like strips (Figure 5.4) to full coverage. The designs may incorporate any of various motifs. Animal, floral, and geometric figures are all suitable.

Figure 5.2. A sliding mechanism near the base of the bank is effective and convenient for retaining and removing coins.

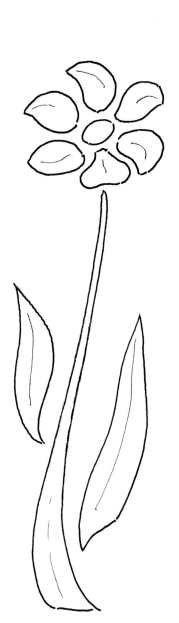

Figure 5.4. Patterns for carving strips in relief frequently incorporate stylized elements in repetitive form.

Figure 5.3. A simple design, such as a single flower, is all the decoration needed when incised on the front surface of a coin bank.

Applique Designs

Instead of decorating flat areas in low relief or by incising, half-round figures and scenes can be carved and glued in place. This practice is particularly good for adding adornment to previously assembled objects. The method of construction follows that recommended for whittling any figure in the round, except for shaping the applique to about half-depth. The backs of appliques and the surfaces to which they are to be glued must be similarly shaped.

A combination of figures comprises the applique in Figure 5.5. The moon is cherry wood, and the stylized ducks are pine—all figures contrasting effectively with the walnut wood. Having a duck's head project into the moon adds a measure of cohesiveness to the scene. A thin coat of quick-setting glue holds the overlays in place. A clear finish protects the assembly.

Figure 5.5. Pine and cherry are the woods used in the carved applique glued onto this walnut-wood bank.

When carving small overlays from thin wood, the procedures normally followed when whittling fully round objects may have to be altered somewhat. Hand holding serves adequately for some woods and applications, but one might try carving thin cutouts while holding them with a long-nose pliers. Some find that a cutting burr in a power tool works best with handheld pieces. Anyway, the result is more important than how the work is done.

A wood recommended for making very thin appliques is tupelo. It is white, strong, tough, and easily carved. In addition, carving it does not produce the fuzziness sometimes resulting when carving basswood.

Another scene suitable as an applique is presented in Figure 5.6, but its application may involve some special steps in construction. The heron's features are styled for half-round carving with little detail, the cattails are to be cut and assembled from dowel rods of two sizes, the leaves are preferably made overlapping, thin, and tapered by whittling, and the base will pass for marsh land or water if made from a strip of weathered barn siding or other rough wood. Normally, overlays are made in the round to about half depth, but the craftsman will find that the thin dowels (cattail stalks) need not be flattened at all. Flattening the large dowels (cattail heads) to the exact point where the small rods enter the large ones will allow the small, round dowels to touch the surface sufficiently for fastening with glue.

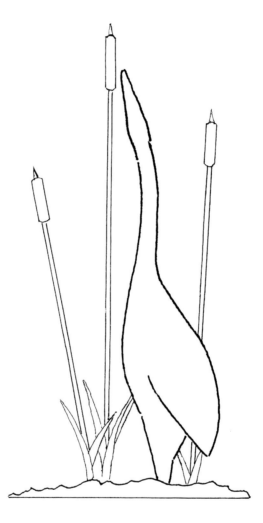

Figure 5.6. A heron, leaves, and base piece, when whittled and assembled with cattails cut from dowel rods, will make an interesting overlay.

Whether to paint or stain an overlay requires thought early in the process. The effect on design can be substantial. There must be sufficient contrast with the wood forming the background of the finished assembly, and the pieces within the applique should be easily distinguished from each other. The use of several species in their natural form usually provides enough contrast, but any coloring intended should be done before gluing the pieces in place. Some craftsmen contend all paints and stains should be thinned and applied sparingly to wood. Doing that will allow the true nature of the base material to be visible in the finished work. Their contention has merit. Unattractively streaked or severely blemished pieces should probably not be used for overlays.

Cylindrical Form

The use of opaque paint is a desirable form of enhancement in some applications. Round banks, being built-up of lengthwise laminates, will sometimes have to be covered to hide the construction lines. The determination of whether or not to apply a solid coat of paint will depend in each case on the wood and the number of laminated pieces used. Visible glue lines are a problem, and any grainy wood or light wood that causes the glue lines to stand out vividly will likely be improved by painting. Laminations not showing such defects, as suggested before, are often preferred when left unpainted.

Embellishment allover with paint is most effective when limited to two or three colors. A bank with acrylic paint covering its exterior in two colors may be seen in Figure 5.7. The narrow V-grooves above and below the chip-carved decoration serve two purposes: to border the design and to aid in obtaining a neat parting line of colors. The bank's bottom (Figure 5.8) shows some of the discoloration in the aspen wood. Paint applied over the visible surface covers both the unsightly dark streaks and the glue lines.

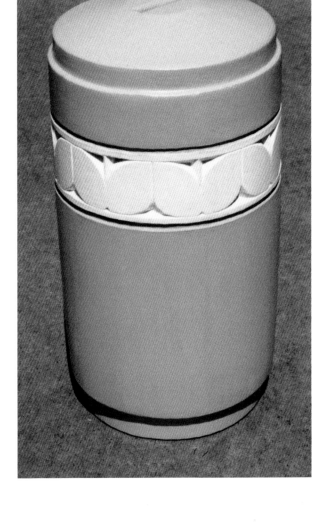

Figure 5.7. The strip design on this neatly chip-carved cylindrical bank has been placed above mid-height for best effect.

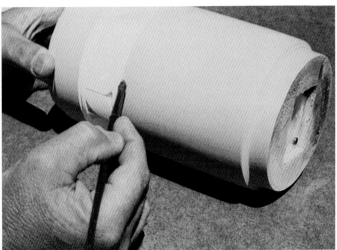

Figure 5.8. Finishing the bank with acrylic paints covers the unsightly glue lines between laminations and dark streaks in the wood.

The bank illustrated is 5 1/2 inches in diameter by 10 inches high. It contains three pieces of aspen cut 2 inches thick, 6 inches wide, and 12 inches long, which have been glued together and turned to shape on a lathe. The chip-carved pattern was laid out and carved after the turning and sanding operations were completed. The slot for receiving coins and the retainer for holding and removing coins at the bottom were also installed after removing the piece from the lathe. The interior cavity for holding them, as must occur with all banks of laminated construction, was made before gluing the three pieces together.

When decorating a cylindrical form, care must be taken to firmly hold the piece without damaging the carved elements. One way to accomplish that is to do the carving before removing the article from the lathe. With the piece firmly clamped between the lathe's live and dead centers, the piece can be easily rotated for working about the bank's circumference. The drawing of the carving also can be accomplished with the piece in the lathe. This preliminary step can be readily carried out if circumferential spacing and sizes are first laid out on a strip of paper.

The finished example also illustrates important points relative to a design's detail, size, and placement. A well-designed carving imparts to the item a better overall appearance than the piece would have if left plain or if tooled excessively. From an artistic point of view, something will often be better than nothing and simplicity will usually be superior to elaborateness. Placement of a strip above, rather than on or a bit below the midpoint, similarly constitutes a major factor in a layout. The reason seems obvious to an artistic eye.

Unlike rectangular box banks, each of which has an internal cavity formed upon assembling its shell of thin boards, cylindrical banks must have a central area hollowed out by sawing or carving thick pieces before gluing them together. Figure 5.9 shows a band saw in use for cutting out a centerpiece for this purpose. The saw blade is directed into the midsection at the bottom. The slot resulting will be replaced by a larger opening for removing coins. Generally, large cylindrical banks and those made of thin boards will require several hollow pieces glued together for the center section.

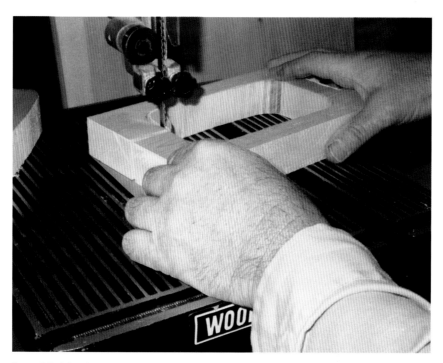

Figure 5.9. A band saw is useful for hollowing interior sections of some cylindrical forms of built-up coin banks.

Animal Figures

As with cylindrical banks, those given the appearance of animals must have a central section removed by sawing or by carving thick pieces. Some of the containers will need several such pieces laminated together to form the inside. The thickness needed for an interior lamination, as well as that of members to be glued to the outside, depends essentially on the size of the finished application and the depth of carving intended.

Figure 5.10 shows a bank carved in the form of an owl. When side-lighted, the owl's more or less eerie features stand out. This shadowy feature lends interest to the piece. It could very well be the reason a youngster would want such a bank for his or her own.

Figure 5.10. A coin receptacle carved like this eerie owl may be most appreciated in a youngster's room.

The bank was made by gluing together two pieces of 2 x 6 spruce construction lumber 12 inches long. The base was then made larger by gluing on two small pieces. Only the large back piece was sawed completely through in this application—the front piece having been routed to half thickness.

The top, as in other banks, contains a slot for receiving coins. One can be easily cut by centering 3/32-inch deep dadoes at corresponding locations in each of the two pieces before gluing them together. A slot may also be formed after the parts are assembled. That procedure follows the steps given for slotting box banks.

As shown in Figure 5.11, a plastic retainer fastened to the bank's back makes possible the viewing of quantities of coins. This arrangement also restricts the removal of coins. A cover fastened so securely obviously impedes quick access to the inside. This impediment could be good or bad. It might be desirable for some persons, but it could be an occasional nuisance for others. Nevertheless, being able to view the interior through a clear plastic sheet without having to turn the bank over will often be considered an asset worth having despite the inconvenience of removing a number of screws in order to take out the coins.

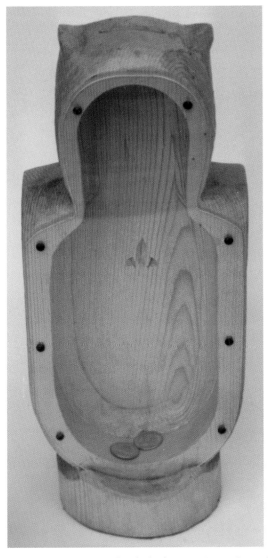

Figure 5.11. Clear plastic screwed to the back permits instant inspection while limiting accessibility a bit more than does a freely sliding retainer.

The construction and finishing processes used definitely affect appearance. The shaping of external details occurs as in Figure 5.12, with the sketching, whittling, and gouging operations following the sawing and assembling of parts. While the laminations are slightly visible upon closely inspecting the sides of the finished assembly, the glue line has little prominence due to having used wood with homogeneous grain and having textured the surfaces with a small gouge. Those facts add support for the item being finished with clear coats of satin polyurethane. As with many articles, allowing the natural grain of the wood to remain visible becomes an overriding consideration.

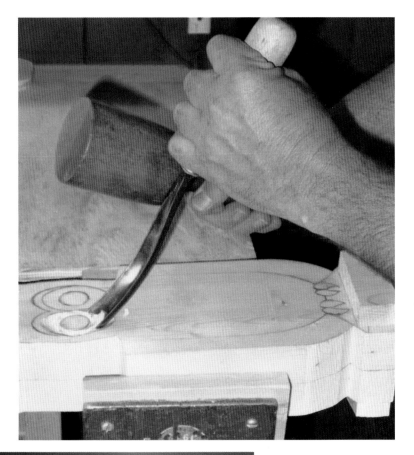

Figure 5.12. The carving of the bank's external features follows the sawing, routing, and assembling operations.

Figure 5.13. Two pieces of 4 x 4 redwood were shaped and assembled for receiving coins before giving the outside the stylized features of an elephant.

Another two-piece bank whose point of lamination cannot be readily seen, except by close inspection, occurs in a carving made in the form of an elephant. Figure 5.13 shows the stylized bank in side view. The line where the pieces of 4 x 4 x 12-inch redwood are glued together extends vertically on center behind the elephant's ear and onto the coin slot on top. The bank seems almost as if it has been made in one piece.

Although subtly tooled, the bank's outside surface has an unmistakable form. Shallow details—some parts smooth, some parts textured—provide the appropriate effect. Here, again, a clear, satin finish protects against damage and discoloration.

Figure 5.14, with the bank on its side, reveals other aspects of construction. The elephant's features are very shallow, indeed. Still they leave no doubt as to what they represent. Also visible on the bank's base are details of a method of retaining coins briefly noted before. Four screws hold a square of plastic in place in this one. Additionally, pieces of felt added to the bottom help eliminate the possibility of scuffing furniture. The use of felt in this way constitutes a practice worth duplicating on banks of all kinds.

A major operation to be carried out before gluing the pieces together and carving the outside is the process of hollowing the inside. As in Figure 5.15, gouges driven by mallet are used in the process. Both halves, meaning each piece of redwood, must have a central portion removed. Care must be exercised in this process to allow for carving the external features. A caliper will assist in maintaining a sufficient thickness of material for this purpose. The drilling of a coin slot, the cutting of an opening for removing coins, and the shaping of a seat for attaching a coin-retaining plate occur after gluing the two hollow sections together. The carving on the outside occurs thereafter.

Figure 5.14. This view of the bank shows more of the shallow detailing and another method of retaining coins and gaining access to them.

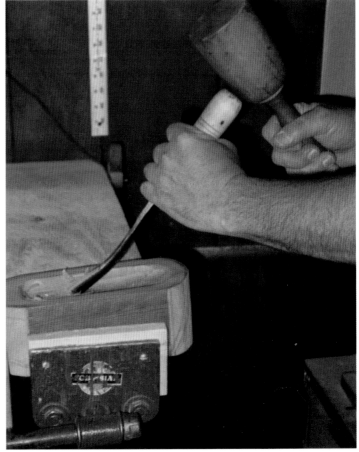

Figure 5.15. The hollowing of pieces must be constantly gauged to avoid cutting the sides too thin for subsequently shaping outside details.

One more method of retaining and removing coins may be specified in a bank's design. This method makes use of a large cork stopper, preferably 1 1/2 inches in diameter or larger. A hole saw of the proper diameter will handily cut an opening for the cork in the base of the finished form. The drawing for carving a piggy bank (Figure 5.16) contains a retainer of the kind described.

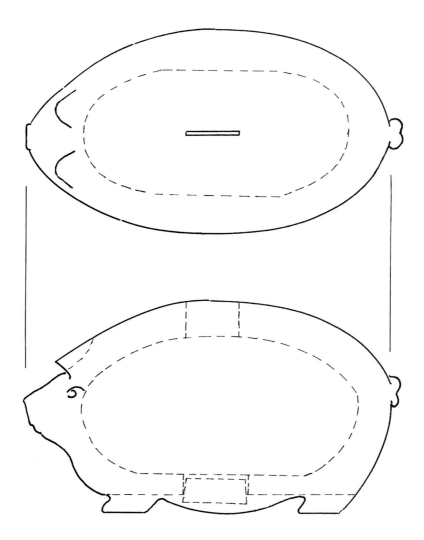

Figure 5.16. A piggy bank with a cork stopper, as drawn, must be made in two or more pieces to allow for hollowing the central area.

Construction of a piggy bank similar to that illustrated begins by selecting or building up an internal section of wood having dimensions about 3 1/2 inches thick, 7 inches high, and 12 inches long. This piece forms the central, lengthwise part of the bank. It must be hollowed to the shape indicated by the dotted lines. Next, two pieces of 1-inch stock are laminated to the sides. The final shaping of the bank then proceeds by sawing and carving in the way that solid three-dimensional figures are customarily shaped. With a little extra effort, a person experienced in carving objects in the round can produce objects like this that have a useful purpose.

The applications in this chapter indicate how fundamentally important design is in construction. Decisions relative to a coin holder's size, type, and functioning are matters of design. Esthetic matters are equally basic, for decisions about form, style, and decorative application also occur at this stage. The wood to be used and the manner of carving enter into those decisions, as well, and all involve decisions in preparation for construction.

Chapter Six
Carving Bowls and Trays

The utilitarian purpose of woodcarving could not be made more evident than occurs when shaping the internal and external features of a bowl or tray. The woodcarver often assumes complete responsibility in applications of this kind. The work then remains entirely under his or her control, from design to finish, with the usefulness and appearance of the product dependent on the quality of the design and skill in carving.

Not all bowls and trays are created by carving. Some are manufactured by other means, with any carved detail added for no purpose other than to decorate. Several such decorative examples are presented later. Designs in a special form of relief are among them.

Utility with Style

The basic objective in fashioning a wooden bowl or tray is to make it practical. This means the piece should do effectively what the designer intends for it to do. An application designed to hold candy or shelled nuts, for example, must be made large and deep enough to hold a reasonable quantity of the item but not so large and deep that it would be more appropriate for conveying pretzels or apples to a group of people. Moreover, it should be light in weight, be easy to hold, be comfortable to carry, be easy to clean, and when placed at rest, be solidly stable. It should have no dangerously pointed or sharp edges, should have no creases or grooves that are difficult to clean, and should not be delicately thin or have projections which could be easily broken. It should provide easy access when loading quantities of the item and removing a few at a time. Also, its surface should be adequately protected to minimize scratching or denting and to withstand occasional washing. The practical considerations necessary to produce a properly functioning article are truly substantial. Indeed, even the choice of wood may have a bearing on the final outcome.

The second objective in designing a bowl or tray, though more properly considered at the time of implementing the first one, is to achieve an esthetically pleasing result. Individual tastes range as widely as levels of sophistication. What excites one person might not please another. Nevertheless, matters of art relative to a product's lines, form, mass, and color deserve serious attention. The visual impact woodcarvings create cannot be ignored, as appearance has a definite bearing on a piece's acceptance. A good designer will always attempt to create a useful object in a distinctively pleasing mode.

Creating Form

Bowls and trays that are shaped by carving can be made from almost any solid wood. Softwoods, hardwoods, light woods, and dark woods are all generally acceptable. Each will respond to the thrust of gouges (Figures 6.1 and 6.2). Woods not recommended include those with highly figured grain and others that have reached some stage of decay or discoloration. For many applications, knotty pieces and thin boards are also undesirable. Sections thick enough to produce the object in one clear piece are most desired. Large billets of wood cut for the fireplace will often do.

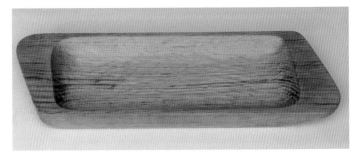

Figure 6.1. The primary considerations in designing a tray, such as this one of pine, are factors pertaining to the article's utility.

Figure 6.2. The carving of bowls and trays can be most readily accomplished by driving the gouges with a mallet.

Before proceeding to carve, details of the design must be worked out in order to select wood of adequate size. A thickness great enough to accommodate the article's depth is one concern. Inspiration for the design is another. The photographs in this chapter indicate how certain designs are derived. The 1 3/8 x 5 3/8 x 16-inch pine tray, for instance, is basically nonrepresentational in design, being somewhat geometric in its distribution of halves, while the 2 x 6 x 7-inch catalpa tray presented in Figure 6.3 emulates a sea shell of a particular type. The symmetry of the pieces is readily apparent.

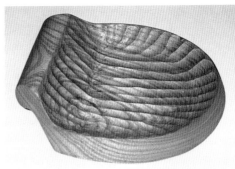

Figure 6.3. This shell-like catalpa tray is an example of a natural body's influence on form in design.

Geometric constructions appeal to many individuals, because the shapes ordinarily display qualities of balance and order. A particularly interesting form is the oval. It is the shape a group of knowledgeable artists chose many years ago to be the most pleasing of all geometric figures—its continuously variable outline being noted as the reason. Be that as it may, the figure can be worked into an interesting bowl. Some techniques applicable in designing and sizing during the initial stages of developing an oval bowl are indicated in the accompanying photographs.

After choosing or creating the design, the steps in creating an article of the kind discussed include (1) planing the wood to the appropriate thickness (Figure 6.4), (2) outlining the article's top edge on the wood (Figure 6.5), (3) sawing along the outline (Figure 6.6), (4) carving the inside areas, (5) shaping the outside, (6) sanding, and (7) applying a finish. Step 3 requires a brief explanation. The edge sawed along the outline should make a 90-degree angle with the top surface, the reason being to provide a vertical surface for propping squarely against the jig when driving the gouge. An angled cut could create problems. The sawed edge will be reshaped after the inside areas have been carved and the piece is turned over for carving the outside.

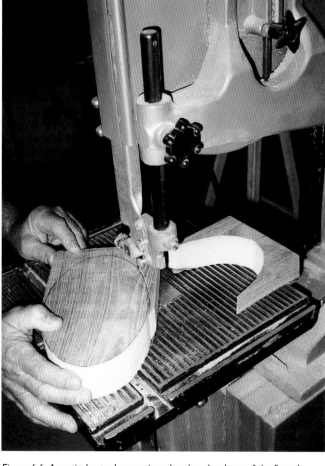

Figure 6.6. A vertical cut when sawing a bowl to the shape of the figure's outline produces an edge that will prop solidly against the carving jig.

Figure 6.4. For use in bowl construction, a billet should be thick enough when surfaced to accommodate the finished article's height in one piece.

The shell of an oval bowl may be most easily carved if curved. The curvatures will be apparent when viewing the piece from above and sideways. Arcs of the oval are suggested. Figure 6.7 illustrates alternate shapes for the sides. The base on which the bowl will rest remains straight and flat. Stability constitutes the designer's main concern when sizing that area.

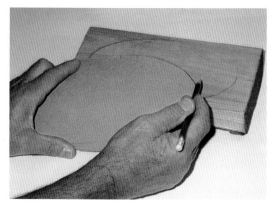

Figure 6.5. A template in the shape of one or two quadrants of the oval can be flipped over for drawing the figure completely and uniformly.

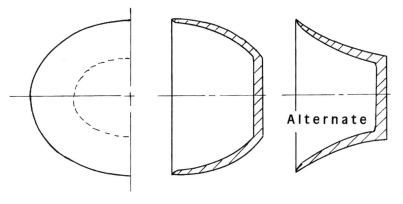

Figure 6.7. When the bowl has been shaped as suggested, the oval, or some part of it, may be seen from any angle.

Some way to gauge and control the thickness of a piece's shell during the carving process must be utilized. Depth drilling and use of a caliper are two workable means. Holes drilled with a Forstner™ bit to limit the depth of gouging, as in Figure 6.8, will help assure the wood will not be carved too thin at the bottom. A 3/8-inch thickness there and thinner sections in other parts of the shell will prove adequate for most woods carved into articles of approximately 2 x 6 x 11-inch dimensions. A deep bowl requires greater thickness. Thickness, customarily, is determined on the basis of an article's size and to a lesser extent on the wood's strength. Judgment enters into individual determinations.

Figure 6.8. A few holes bored to the proper depth will serve as a gauge when shaping inside areas of a bowl.

Representational Shapes

Designs for bowls and trays are sometimes based on plant growth. Leaves are a good source. When stylized, as in forming the catalpa nut bowl (Figures 6.9 and 6.10), the result is both an interesting and useful piece. Because of the ease in carving catalpa, it can be quickly pared smooth with a nearly flat gouge before sanding the surface to its final smoothness. Catalpa is excellent for this article, just as it is for others that do not contain intricate details.

Figure 6.9. Foliage is an excellent source of inspiration for design, as in this smooth catalpa tray.

Figure 6.10. A tray must have a base of sufficient size to provide stability, and the bottom surface is a good place for the craftsman's personal symbol.

A bowl of similar representation, though of different wood and texture, is pictured in Figure 6.11. The walnut wood used in the 2 x 7 1/2 x 11-inch bowl makes an attractive and substantial piece, but it requires more force in gouging than the softer woods. Its interior surface may be pared smooth or be left with gouge marks showing. There are those who prefer to see the texture gouging causes, which is a matter to be considered when designing a gift for someone of that inclination.

Figure 6.11. Whether a bowl's interior shall be smoothed or be left with a pattern of tool marks is essentially a matter of individual choice.

By stylizing, a designer has the freedom to represent leaves in more than one way. A two-compartment shape may be seen in Figure 6.12. Its size is 2 x 5 1/2 x 12 inches. This design, as holds true for others to be made into bowls or trays, may be adapted in size to suit the article's purpose. Once, again, a need to analyze and accommodate specific utilitarian requirements enters into the product's design.

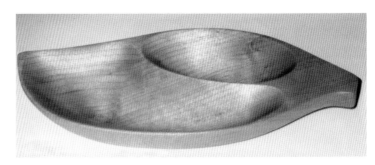

Figure 6.12. A stylized leaf design with two compartments is easily carved in butternut and also makes a useful container for snack food.

Figure 6.13 contains more forms of a representational type. The designs are based on symbols familiar to card players everywhere. One seemingly appropriate application is the construction of shallow trays for distributing snacks among an assembly of card-playing guests. Carved as shown, the trays would likely bring forth some very favorable observations.

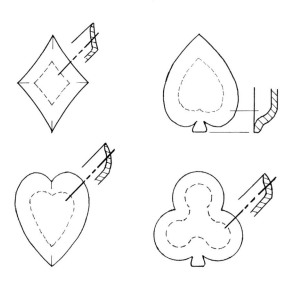

Figure 6.13. Snack trays shaped as these drawings indicate are most likely to impress card players.

or other snack foods. Acceptance of an abstraction like this is often contingent on a visual assessment of the form, while concerns about how effectively distributions of line and mass augment the tray's physical needs sometimes receive little attention. A complete evaluation takes both the practical and esthetic aspects of design into account.

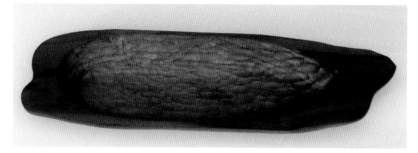

Figure 6.14. Not all trays and bowls must be outlined in a tangible form, as indicated by this nonrepresentational contour.

Additional shapes that do not represent anything, perhaps, other than their use to hold food, are shown in Figures 6.15 and 6.16. The catalpa bowl has dimensions overall of 2 3/4 x 5 1/2 x 9 1/2 inches, and the small mahogany dish is 3/4 x 4 x 5 1/2 inches in size. As with all other articles presented in this chapter, the final shapes of these examples are the result of gouging and hand sanding.

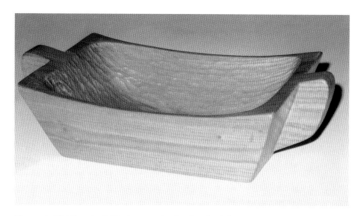

Figure 6.15. Many individuals seem inclined to look for representational features in a design, even if the designer did not intend such.

While this application leaves little room for originality, it does exemplify how powerful a design can be if it relates to someone or represents something familiar to the observer. Nonrepresentational creations seldom provide associations of this kind.

Nonrepresentational Shapes

All nonrepresentational art, in some instances called "abstract art," has a common thread of being conceived apart from concrete reality. Formal aspects of art are the basis of such designs, with their evaluation centering on matters of line, mass, and color. The principles of balance, rhythm, variety, coherence, and so forth, also enter into considerations of the esthetic quality involved in each composition. Nothing tangible exists as a source of inspiration at the time of creation. Therein lies what many consider to be a strength of nonrepresentational design. The designer remains free and unfettered to do original work.

The foremost concern in product design continues to be an object's utility, regardless of whether it does or does not represent something. A tray or bowl must, therefore, be given substance appropriate for accomplishing a particular purpose. The determinations involved in doing that tend to dictate matters of form, but they do not restrict the designer from arranging elements either to represent something, such as playing-card symbols, or to have no particular point of reference.

The 1 1/2 x 5 x 16-inch walnut tray shown in Figure 6.14 is an example in which the outlined form does not duplicate anything in particular. The shape definitely has a visual impact. It also has a bearing on the requirements for holding and distributing cookies

Figure 6.16. To keep weight and size relative, the mahogany wood in this 4 x 5-inch shelled-peanut tray was carved to a thickness of 3/16 of an inch.

Additional suggestions for shaping bowls and trays are given in Figure 6.17. The drawings are top-view outlines which may be copied and adjusted in size as seen fit for an item at hand. All are intended for articles of one-piece construction.

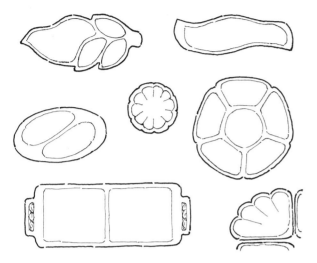

Figure 6.17. These sketched shapes indicate some of the variations that can be incorporated in designs for carving bowls and trays.

Adding Decoration

Unlike the previous applications in which the artwork is integrated with construction, the articles illustrated in this section contain carved features which are decorative additions. Their use has little bearing on an article's shape. They are applied for reasons of artistic enhancement.

Two kinds of trays are included here. One is a flat serving tray with handles attached to the ends, and the other is a carved piece with flat areas in two corners. Both contain a style of carving which, while not frequently observed in use, can produce very effective decorations on utilitarian items.

A serving tray is shown in Figure 6.18. The 11 1/2 x 23-inch pine server has an overall height of 1 1/8 inches at places other than the handles. A 1/2-inch thick piece forms the part of the base containing the carved decoration. Its thickness is not the reason for the shallow carving, however. Applications of this kind require decorations that can be easily cleaned.

Figure 6.18. A carving in plane relief is the most practical form of carved decoration for the type of tray shown here.

In addition to being made shallow, the details of a carving on a tray should not be highly contoured. As shown in Figure 6.19, the design can be left almost entirely flat. The result is a form of carving called "plane relief" or "plane carving." Most of the features are left in the original plane of the board's surface. This type of design has the advantage of being easily completed, as an object's features are defined with only a limited amount of detailing. Nonetheless, the simple detailing adds considerably to a item's appearance.

Figure 6.19. Shallow carving, flat-faced figures, and a stippled background are the hallmark of plane carving.

A close observer will notice the similarity of carving in plane relief to outline carving. They are alike in two ways: both are begun by incising along drawn outlines and both eventually produce figures in a plane. Their similarity ends when the background of one is recessed to make the features stand out.

Efforts to create a smooth background in relief carving by ordinary methods of tooling can cause problems. This holds especially true when attempting to carve in very low relief. A recommended procedure for carving a decoration like that shown is to incise around the fruit and leaves, then gouge away the background to a depth of about 3/32 of an inch. A flat, or nearly flat, tool works best. The unevenness occurring can be obliterated later by stippling the entire background area. A common nail does a nice job for this purpose if first ground to a uniform point.

Another application of plane carving may be seen in Figure 6.20. In this instance, small, floral carvings decorate two corners of a tray which, too, has been carved. The cherry wood in this item is 7 inches square and 7/8 of an inch thick. The result is a tray that not only functions as desired but also one that creates visual interest.

Figure 6.20. A carved candy dish like this can also be further enhanced with small decorative carvings.

For carving bowls and trays, cherry wood serves beautifully. A design's carved details define sharply in the firm wood, and they maintain their sharpness through much handling. Cherry has a richness of color, as well, turning reddish with age. It is almost without equal for items requiring a durable wood without a porous grain.

Chapter Seven
Sculpting Spoons, Stirrers, and Scoops

The items presented in this chapter have value as items of practical necessity. Everywhere cooking is done one will find stirring spoons and spatulas in use, and wherever small quantities of granular material are being parceled out, a scoop will come in handy. Many of the articles have distinct advantages when fashioned from wood. Even a water dipper, though such devices are not as commonly used in homes today as in times past, will be more suitable for certain applications when sculpted from wood than if constructed in another material. How the woodcarver can make these items flawlessly useful and artistically acceptable remains the objective in the sections that follow.

Practical Tooling

Handheld devices of the kind being considered here may be made from kiln-dried lumber, tree trunks, or fallen limbs. Naturally dried parts of a tree taken directly from the forest or the woodpile may, in fact, be preferred for some applications to clear, straight pieces bought at a lumber mill. For example, a spatula or stirrer to be made with a curved handle will be strongest if split from a piece of wood as shown in Figure 7.1. A straight piece sawed on a curve might actually be weak because of the cross-grain produced.

The grain in the wood selected for any item having a straight, long handle should run lengthwise, as well, and for use in cooking, the wood should not be soft. Many nonporous, firm woods will do. Maple and cherry are suitable. The general message, in any case, is to analyze requirements and choose whatever will work for the particular application.

Alternatives also exist in the choice and use of tools and equipment. Tools commonly identified as carpenter's implements, rather than belonging to the woodcarver, will be used in this work. Spokeshaves and drawknives are among them. They are used in the final shaping of articles. Accompanying explanations of their use is a method to be illustrated later for clamping and holding pieces in a vise with a handscrew while sculpting them to shape. The arrangement takes the place of the old-fashioned shaving bunk once commonly used when shaving spokes for wagon wheels. As will

be seen, the arrangement is somewhat make-shift, yet it does the job effectively. It provides an inexpensive alternative to making or purchasing a shaving bunk. This pragmatic approach for an occasional application might not provide the convenience of the more specialized piece of equipment, but the product—not the process—is the thing of most importance.

Shaping Spatulas and Stirrers

The process of designing wooden implements for use in cooking involves the basic steps relevant to designing utilitarian objects of all kinds. They are: (1) defining the purpose, (2) analyzing requirements, and (3) preparing a drawing. If the need is for a device for stirring broth or blending mixtures in a deep pot, a long, straight-handled shaft with a broad end will prove useful. A spoon-like shape with a hole in the end might be perfect for the task. If, on the other hand, a device is needed for mixing chopped food in a shallow pan, a less broad stirrer with a curved handle could be exactly what one needs. Strength sufficient to withstand pressure without being heavy, thick, and cumbersome to hold, a tight grain and a smooth surface for ease in cleaning, and a handle long enough to keep one's hand away from the heated substances are other important considerations. It is to be noted in passing that wooden utensils can be used without fear of damaging the thin, slick coatings applied to the inside of pots and pans today. The utensils have the further advantage of not denting the metal when being rapped, as cooks often do, on the edge of a pot between periods of stirring the contents.

Once the pertinent factors are analyzed and point to a satisfactory form for the device, several potential solutions are sketched on paper. The best is chosen for the item. Full-size drawings are needed for shapes intended to be transferred to the wood by tracing.

As to dimensions, spatulas and stirrers will generally be sufficiently thick if tapered from a sharp end up to about 3/4 of an inch at the handgrip. In width, the widest parts for stirring will vary from about 2 to 3 1/2 inches across. Lengths also vary. End-to-end measurements of 10 to 13 inches are common.

Figure 7.1. Pieces split from billets like this one are superior for making spatulas and stirrers with curved handles.

Construction proceeds after obtaining wood having the characteristics needed. Any planing to thickness must be done at this point and prior to outlining the article's shape on the wood. The shaping process begins by sawing about the article's profile on a band saw (Figure 7.2) or scroll saw, followed by shaving the handle to shape with a spokeshave (Figure 7.3). Any gouging needed (Figure 7.4) occurs after roughing in the handle. The boring of the hole in the stirrer shown may occur at any point in the shaping process.

Figure 7.2. Flat boards of cherry wood serve well for stirrers that are relatively straight from end to end.

Figure 7.3. A spokeshave is a practical tool for sculpting long handles to the smoothness and shape desired.

Figure 7.4. The concave carving of this stirrer's cupped end should be shallow.

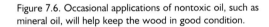

Unlike areas covered with decorative carvings, carved objects of this kind may be sanded thoroughly. Drum sanders of various grits in a drill press, as in Figure 7.5, are very helpful for smoothing curvatures.

What is the appropriate finishing material? Spatulas, stirrers, and similar articles are best given either a finish of nontoxic oil or none at all. For occasional application, mineral oil or vegetable oils that will not become rancid are recommended (Figure 7.6). Protection from the effects of frequent washing is a principal concern.

Figure 7.5. Drum sanders equipped with sleeves of progressively finer grits expedite the smoothing process.

Figure 7.6. Occasional applications of nontoxic oil, such as mineral oil, will help keep the wood in good condition.

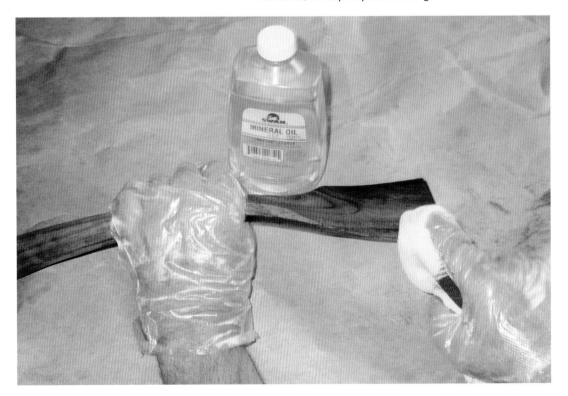

Three wooden utensils are shown in Figure 7.7. The different shapes indicate the freedom possible in design. The forms are also a product of the utility involved. All can be used for stirring and scraping, but the piece with the broad end serves principally as a spatula for turning eggs and hamburgers in a frying pan. While a "lollipop" shape could be made into a practical utensil for stirring liquid foods, it is obvious from the stirrer at the top of the picture that more interesting features can be achieved by carving than would be possible by making a simple, but workable, circular piece at the end of a round stick.

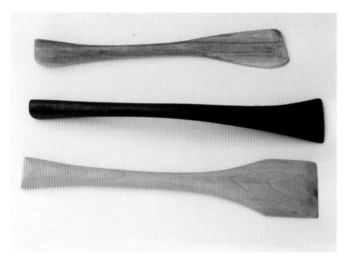

Figure 7.7. Spatula and stirrer designs can be far more appealing than those manufactured with handles shaped like dowel rods.

The walnut piece of modern design, which is shown again in Figure 7.8 to reveal its curvature, has a form made specifically for mixing hot stir-fries in a shallow pan. This piece has a continuous bow throughout its 13 1/2-inch length, arching a full 1 1/2 inches at its center. The convenience and strength of an article split from a curved section of wood, as this one has been, soon becomes apparent to anyone stirring food in a skillet over a hot stove. Provision for firm gripping is another feature worked into the design.

Shaping and Decorating Handles

The design of a handle for a wooden utensil may take any of various forms. A major requirement in each instance is to give the implement a shape that can be comfortably held and which does not easily slip or twist from one's grasp. Increasing the handle's thickness appropriately toward the end will help in this matter. In the process, attention must be centered on keeping the utensil's overall thickness, hence its weight, to a reasonable minimum. The several shapes previously illustrated offer a few of the options possible. Additional designs are included in Figure 7.9.

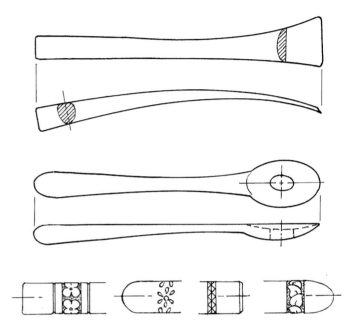

Figure 7.9. These sketches display designs for decorating handles and several utensils that are adequate without such ornamentation.

To assist in gripping and to add a bit more visual appeal, the handles of some servers and stirrers may be decorated with carved details. The decorated handle of the spatula in Figure 7.8 is an acceptable example. Such decorations should be shallow and not too close to the place on the implement where food will normally be handled. Also, they should be positioned where a substantial portion of the design can be easily viewed when not in use.

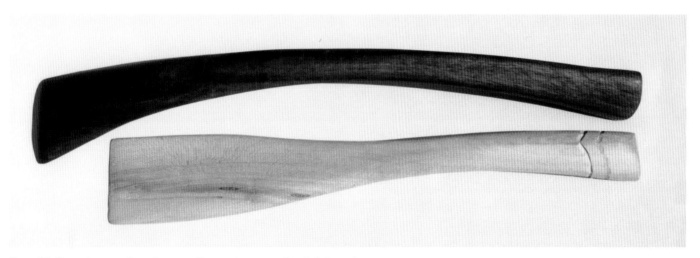

Figure 7.8. Shown here are the walnut utensil's natural curvature for stir-frying and a sycamore spatula with an appropriately placed decoration.

Another example may be seen in Figure 7.10. Side-lighting brings out the carved detail. This small spatula has a 12-inch length, a width varying from 3/4 inch to 2 1/4 inches, and a thickness varying from a sharp edge to 7/8 of an inch at the handle's tip. How the chip-carved pattern conforms to the shape of the handle is worthy of attention.

Figure 7.10. Light directed from the side brings out the lengthwise chip-carved decoration on the handle of this maple-wood piece.

Examples of other patterns are included in Figure 7.9. Particularly noteworthy are the decorative designs for incising and carving in plane relief. Being small and intended for shallow carving, the designs are ideal for stippling the background areas. Simple, repetitive patterns encircling the handles of the items are recommended for those designing decorations of their own. Of importance in this regard is first to make sure the object to be decorated works as effectively as intended.

Salad Server Design

Salad servers consist of a spoon and a fork, but not in the conventional sense. Neither has the shape of utensils made for eating. Their sole purpose is for clamping about bunches of salad greens and distributing them among individual servers. Considerable freedom in their design is possible. The pair shown in Figure 7.11 illustrates this fact. Each is 12 inches long, 2 1/2 inches wide at one end and 1 1/8 inches at the other. They are 5/8 of an inch thick, except in the central area where the thickness is 7/16 of an inch.

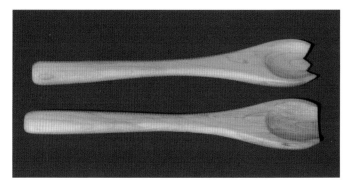

Figure 7.11. A fork-and-spoon combination in maple has an interesting and practical form when designed as shown.

Nearly everything mentioned for designing stirrers applies to salad servers. Exceptions occur in two ways, however. One way has to do with the manner in which the handles are gripped when being used, and the other applies to the ends for gathering and clamping the loose vegetables. The needs resulting from this analysis are straightness from end to end and a slight cupping at the working end. By making one utensil saw-toothed, the jagged tip will assist when gathering the leafy material together. Whether or not to carve small decorations into the servers' handles is essentially a matter of personal choice. Of course, when that is done the decorations on the two should be a matching pair.

Designing Scoops and Dippers

Anyone dishing out dry, granular material, such as grain for birds and bulk food for a dog, can use a scoop. One sawed, gouged, and whittled from a solid piece of wood to create a form like that shown in Figure 7.12 will be practically indispensable in some homes. The overall dimensions of the basswood piece are 3 x 3 1/2 x 8 inches. Here, again, the handle's design assures a far more substantial grip than made possible by the straight, round handles sometimes fixed on such implements. In all aspects, the piece's form truly derives from its function.

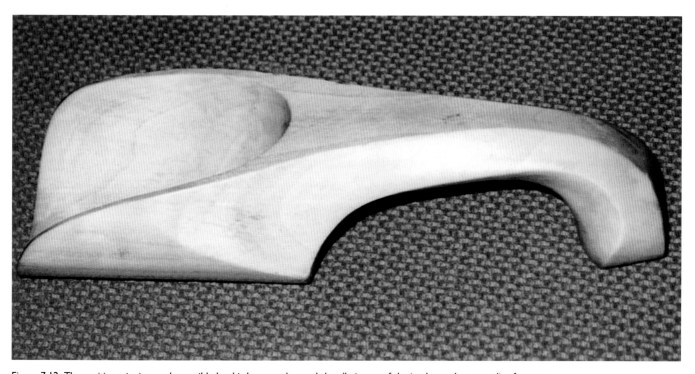

Figure 7.12. The positive gripping made possible by this basswood scoop's handle is one of the implement's outstanding features.

A multi-purpose ladle is pictured in Figure 7.13. Handheld instruments in this form will sometimes be used to dispense dry pet food, grain, and fertilizer—applications which work well with a sturdy device like this—but the ladle's main purpose is for dipping water from a pail and sprinkling it onto potted plants. For most such applications, a piece of stock 2 1/2 inches thick, 3 inches wide, and 11 1/2 inches long will suffice. This size will permit the gouging of a cup over 2 inches deep in the shape of an oval 3 x 4 inches on its top surface, although the dimensions can be readily adjusted to suit special requirements. One advantage of this form of ladle is the strength derived from having one solid piece with the grain running straight throughout the length. Its disadvantage, though not always a serious one, may be realized when having to tip a bag or bucket in order to extract the contents.

Figure 7.13. An object fashioned as shown will sometimes be used as both a scoop and a dipper about the home.

An article for dipping and dispensing water that has been assembled from two pieces is shown hanging in the sauna where it has been used extensively over steaming, hot rocks (Figure 7.14). Its 15-inch length contains a cup 3 3/8 inches, maximum diameter, by 3 inches deep. The handle's tapered profile serves effectively for holding and hanging while being light in weight. Cup and handle are securely joined with a small mortise and tenon, and several coats of an exterior grade polyurethane offer considerable protection. The full advantages of the dipper's design may be reviewed in Chapter 1.

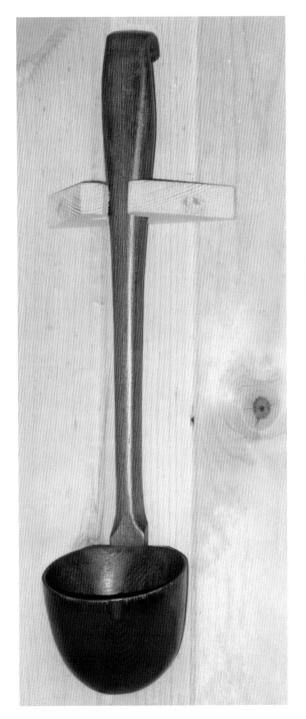

Figure 7.14. This dipper has been designed specifically for sprinkling water over heated stones in a sauna, where it is used extensively.

For comparison, a similar article made in one piece is shown in Figure 7.15. Its 17-inch length contains a 3 1/2-inch deep by 3-inch diameter cup. Dippers of this type have distinct advantages when fashioned from forked tree limbs. A piece of wood like the one in Figure 7.16 will suffice, provided that surface decay (as indicated by the growth of fungus) has not progressed too far into the heartwood. The manner of cutting the dipper from the wood is presented in Figure 7.17. The dipper's strength derives from the tough crotch wood in the cup and the wood's straight grain being lengthwise in the handle. Although the gouging and whittling of solid crotch wood can be somewhat difficult, the figured grain in that part of a tree generally makes a very strong and durable dipper.

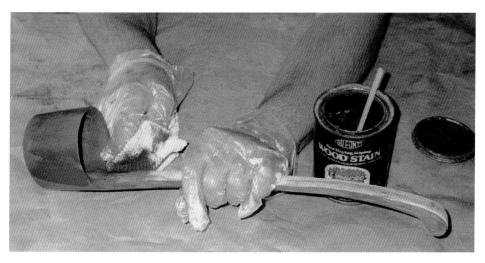

Figure 7.15. A one-piece dipper sculptured from a branch where it was attached to the tree's crotch has strength not often obtainable when using other wood.

Figure 7.16. A Y-branch such as this can be used to make a dipper if decay – as indicated by the fungus on the bark – has not progressed into the heartwood.

Figure 7.17. The dashed line defines the position for sawing out a dipper in order to take advantage of the wood's grain in the crotch and limb.

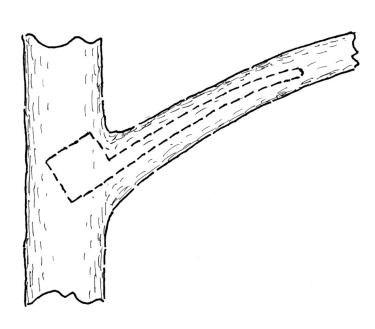

There are two suggestions to be made relative to constructing such an item. One has to do with clamping the piece for shaping after roughing out its outline on the band saw. In the absence of a shaving bunk, an inexpensive arrangement like that shown in Figure 7.18 will prove helpful. Clamping the piece in the vise without the use of the hand clamp would be difficult. Whether to use a spokeshave or a drawknife to do the shaping remains a matter of choice, regardless of the method of clamping.

Figure 7.18. Clamping as shown is a pragmatic alternative to the shaving bunk for many who only occasionally sculpt long-handled articles.

The second point, the final one to be considered here, pertains to the shaping of the cup. During the roughing-in stage, it is advisable to bore a hole toward the cup's center (Figure 7.19). This hole should be bored to the depth to which the cavity will be carved. It then serves as a depth gauge, which will be an asset when enlarging the cavity. How the cup will be finished is also a matter of personal preference. Power carving and hand carving with gouges and mallet are equally acceptable, just as is true for power sanding or hand sanding. In the words of the vernacular, there is more than one way to skin the cat. This simply implies that the result continues to be the thing of greatest importance, for the finished piece is the primary subject of scrutiny and evaluation over time.

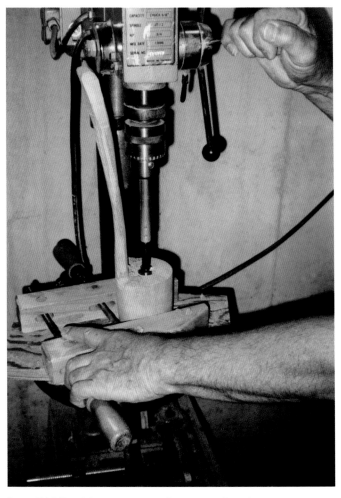

Figure 7.19. Depth boring to prepare for carving a dipper's cup may occur at any point in the roughing-in process.

Chapter Eight
Crafting Useful Tableware

Articles useful at the dinner table serve various purposes, and they can add both charm and interest to the setting if carved from wood. Imagine this scene in the home of a woodcarver: Guests about to be seated for dinner first observe a pair of sumac candlesticks carved in counterpoised spirals to reveal a beautiful golden grain, then their attention focuses on the clever little creatures holding cards that denote where each shall sit. Before long, they scrutinize the carved napkin rings, the small dish sculpted for serving appetizers, the neatly fashioned wooden salad bowls and servers, the cherry board suitably shaped for use in cutting bread, and at the end of the meal, the leaf-like tray of mints and the exquisite toothpick holder being passed about. What woodcarver would want to miss the conversation stimulated by these items?

The Warmth of Wood

As this contrived scene suggests, wood still has many uses at the table. The material is not made into utensils and containers as often as in times past, but opportunities to replace manufactured ware with individually crafted woodcarvings are ever-present. The warmth of wood may be just what is needed to offset the sleek metallic glitz and glazed ceramic sheen so common in table settings today. Then, too, the carved aspect of the creations might heighten personal interest and appeal.

Handcrafted pieces sometimes have a special quality. For illustration, consider the design of a tray for passing a small portion of hors d'oeuvres about the table. What could be more appealing and appropriate than to give a container intended for distributing chunks of smoked salmon or dried oysters the simplified shape of a fish? Figure 8.1 shows a tray carved for just such a purpose. Its overall dimensions are 7/8 x 4 x 9 1/2 inches, which makes a suitable server for a group of several people. This size can be readily adjusted for individual purposes without adversely affecting the relationship between the container's shape and the dish's contents. Design conscious individuals will notice the article's thin curved handle at one end and the flat tapered area at the other. Each contributes to the stylized figure's appearance.

Although the visual impact of form is a concern when creating something for the table, utility must remain the primary concern. Light weight, smoothness to the touch, and ease in holding,

passing, and cleaning are among the considerations. The woodcarver has a responsibility to make the wood respond to the special requirements in constructing articles of this kind. The drawing and sawing operations proceed as for larger trays and bowls, but one step that might be overlooked is the smoothing of the sawed outline before shaping the dish's cavity. Taking this step in reverse order could easily result in a piece being misshapen by, first, having to undercut the drawn perimeter to sand away excessive roughness in some areas and, then, no longer being able to adjust the cavity to obtain the thicknesses of wood and sizes of flat areas along the tray's edge as designed. The drum sander shown in Figure 8.2 is positioned for use as recommended. The gouging, whittling, and paring operations can proceed next to the point of sanding the piece.

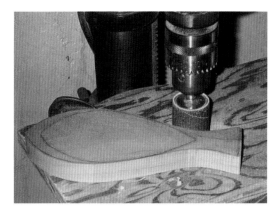

Figure 8.2. Design layout, sawing about the profile, and smoothing the edge are important preparations for carving a dish.

Figure 8.1. A dish stylized as shown, and finished with nontoxic oil, is an impressive way to serve portions of seafood hors d'oeuvres.

Material thickness is always a concern in items of this kind. Small dishes and some large ones made of strong wood may be carved to a thickness no greater than 3/16 of an inch in many areas. However, thicknesses in bottom areas is usually greater than that required elsewhere. An objective is to achieve a comfortable weight level.

A final sanding and an application of mineral oil should be given a tray intended for use as mentioned. These and other details of construction for similar items may be reviewed in Chapter 6.

Something for Guests

A sure way to impress dinner guests is to provide each with a specially made place card and holder. Such additions at the table are often considered to be an unessential extra, and many gatherings in the home are not large enough to necessitate their use. Nevertheless, even in a small group the attention and appeal promoted by hand-carved figures supporting individual name cards can be worth the effort involved. Their use might even create a little excitement among friends.

Place-card holders can be carved in the form of small animals, floral clusters, and inanimate objects. An application is shown in Figure 8.3. Three-dimensional figures in this and other forms are fun to make, and you can rest assured they will be noticed. Figure 8.4 presents a pair of geese that go together in a setting for a related couple. Is there some humor to be derived from the posturing of the two geese? In any case, these several examples are adaptations of full-relief carving to something practical. They are unlike most carvings in the round in that regard, yet like others, they are great stimulants of conversation. Guests appreciate them.

The holders must be appropriately sized. Thicknesses of about 1 1/2 inches, with widths and heights ranging from 2 1/2 to 3 inches, generally suffice for small figures in full relief. A practical consideration to be taken into account in their sizing is to provide for sawing a narrow groove at an appropriate spot for supporting the usual 2 x 3-inch card (Figure 8.5). The slot may be vertical or horizontal, depending on a holder's configuration. Small animals in full relief are usually slotted for receiving a card's side edge. For other holders, such as the one of hearts illustrated in Figure 8.6, a horizontal slot toward the top will often be preferred. The drawings include overall dimensions of the two. A picture of a bunny sized as shown may be seen by returning to Chapter 1. As to the efficacy of the heart-shaped holder, could that be the sort of friendship motif you might want to carry throughout a full set of place-card holders and onto other accessories for use at the table?

Figure 8.5. To be used as a place-card holder, a woodcarving must be designed to receive a narrow saw cut in an appropriate spot.

Figure 8.3. Small carved animals supporting place-cards at the dinner table are likely to impress guests, especially the youngsters present.

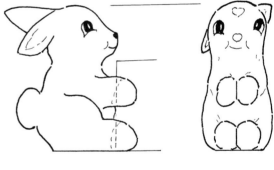

1 1/2 x 3 x 3

Figure 8.4. These cardholders show how some figures of similar kind might be adapted and paired for use at place settings for couples.

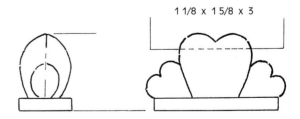

1 1/8 x 1 5/8 x 3

Figure 8.6. The location of a slot for holding a place-card will bear markedly on the figure's position and arrangement.

Whether to color place-card holders or to cover the natural wood with nothing more than a transparent satin finish depends on the manner of carving and its level of sophistication. Color undoubtedly brings out the realistic appearance of naturalistic carvings, and applications of acrylic paint seem appropriate for work having a novel effect, as is generally the case when animals are shaped into holders. Color is also useful for covering bland or unattractively blemished wood. Abstract creations and articles of elegant composition and design, on the other hand, might be given a clear finish if sculptured in mahogany or other wood of substantial quality. The impression one wants to create enters squarely into the decision-making process of what to do, both as regards the style of carving and its finish. An analysis of the specific purpose helps define the outcome.

An application in which the wood alone provides the color is shown in Figure 8.7. Repetitive elements in relief are the only embellishment. The wood selected, the style employed, and the form created combine to achieve the purpose involved. Obviously utilitarian, the carved napkin rings are intended to serve impressively whenever special guests come to dinner.

Figure 8.8. Blanks sawed from a sapling or branch for making napkin rings should be bored on center before carving the outer surface.

Figure 8.7. Napkin rings—these made of mahogany—may be most appreciated when decorated with a symbol of friendship.

Napkin rings of wood are easy to make. Construction begins either by sawing pieces from a dry tree branch or sapling of about 1 3/4 inches diameter or by removing pieces of similar diameter from kiln-dried lumber turned on a lathe. The idea is to form an entire set of the rings at once and to prepare for carving by having side grain occur about each ring's entire outside surface. Sections cut from branch stock have grain running naturally in the direction desired. The length of the pieces to remove depends on the design, but a dimension of 7/8 to 1 1/2 inches will generally do.

Several 1-inch sections sawed from a branch are shown in Figure 8.8. A ring's bark is also being whittled away after having removed wood from the center. By following this sequence of operations, the woodcarver can readily obtain a uniform thickness of wood throughout a ring's circumference. Rings first turned on a lathe do not ordinarily present a problem of this kind.

With a section of wood in hand, a hole is made in its center for holding the cloth napkin. A hole 1 1/4 inches in diameter works well. It can be easily and uniformly constructed with a hole saw (Figure 8.9), but for some woods, this operation might have to be followed by sanding the ring's inside surface on a drum sander.

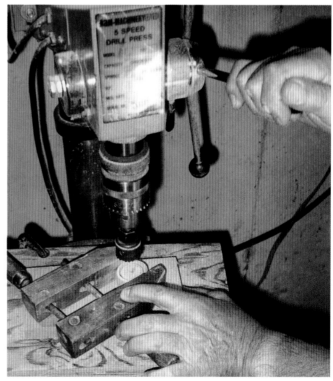

Figure 8.9. A hole saw of 1 1/4 inches diameter is very useful for cutting out the center of a piece to be made into a napkin ring.

The next step consists of penciling the design on the wood to be carved, as in Figure 8.10. The surface decoration is then incised or carved in relief as called for in the design. A piece with a comparatively thin ring is shown being incised with a power-driven burr in Figure 8.11. The hand carving of hearts in relief (Figure 8.12) requires pieces with a thicker ring than the previous one in order to provide for forming the decoration without jeopardizing strength. Adjustments in outside dimensions are sometimes necessary during the design stage to accommodate the decoration.

Figure 8.12. Whatever the manner of decorating, a napkin ring must be sufficiently thick to allow for carving without seriously affecting strength.

Figure 8.10. The napkin ring is ready for decorating after having removed the center and pared the outside surface to accommodate the design.

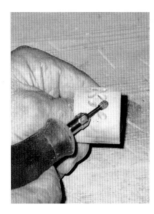

Figure 8.11. Designs may be incised or carved in relief on the rings, using either power-driven cutting burrs or other carving tools.

For After Dinner

Another utilitarian device sometimes enhanced by the addition of a carved decoration is the toothpick holder. Here, again, a cylindrical piece is used. As when making napkin rings, the piece may be taken directly from a round branch or sapling or be sawed from a section of wood turned on a lathe.

One containing a pattern of incised lines and acrylic paint is the subject of Figure 8.13. The holder is bark-covered. It might be most appropriate in a rustic setting, but it does show how a small amount of carving and color can decorate a piece having a natural appearance. The bark is relatively smooth and tight, conditions of considerable importance for items of this kind. Two coats of polyurethane seal the surface.

For convenience in use, a holder must be properly sized. The one pictured has an outside diameter of 1 1/2 inches, a height of 2 1/4 inches, and a hole bored 1 1/2 inches in diameter and 1 7/8 inches deep. It is easy to handle, does not tip over easily, and holds toothpicks in the proper position for ready accessibility. If desired, sizes slightly different from those given can be used without seriously affecting utility.

The internal cavity in a toothpick holder will ordinarily be constructed before carving the outside. A Forstner bit can be used for this purpose (Figure 8.14). Although the marks left at the bottom by this tool will seldom be seen, they can be removed by grinding with an abrading tool (Figure 8.15).

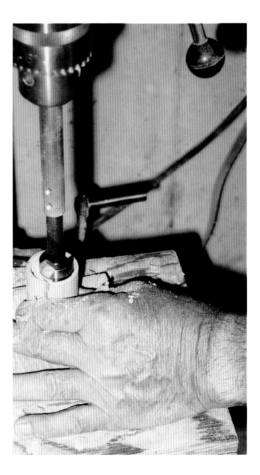

Figure 8.13. A toothpick holder with tight, smooth bark, when embellished with incised lines and colorful paint, can be both useful and attractive.

Figure 8.14. One way to hollow a toothpick holder to the depth and breadth desired is through use of a Forstner™ bit in a drill press.

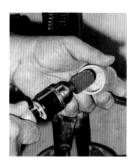

Figure 8.15. An abrading tool can be used to smooth the inside surface of a holder that has been bored out with a Forstner bit.

As shown in Figures 8.16 and 8.17, the relief carving and stippling operations are next in line. Patterns of various configuration are given in Figure 8.18. Many of them are suitable for stippling when the figures are carved in relief. They may be applied to napkin holders as well as to toothpick dispensers.

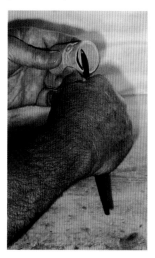

Figure 8.16. Internal shaping and the general shaping of the outside surface normally precede the carving of a toothpick holder.

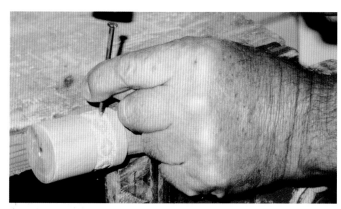

Figure 8.17. A common nail with its point reshaped is a useful tool for stippling the background of small designs in relief.

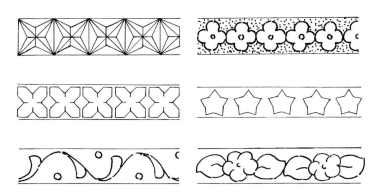

Some items, particularly those with a homogeneous grain, can be improved considerably by staining (Figure 8.19). Stain makes the decoration stand out. In that respect, it serves the same purpose as acrylic paint on a bark-covered holder. A final coating of a clear, satin finish will seal the item. The spraying of polyurethane with the item set inside a carton is one way to apply the finish without causing collateral damage (Figure 8.20).

Figure 8.19. Stain improves appearance by making a carved design stand out prominently, especially on a wood having homogeneous grain.

Figure 8.20. The use of a carton while coating small objects with a spray sealer will help prevent collateral damage.

Figure 8.18. Strip designs like these may be adjusted as necessary for decorating circumferential objects of various kinds and sizes.

Candlesticks and Cutting Boards

A particularly interesting item is a candlestick made from sumac wood in the shape of a spiral. The internal golden grain of sumac as revealed by the whittler's knife has a beauty that few woods can equal (Figure 8.21). The species shown is staghorn sumac, which grows alongside the roadways and open fields in many states. Each of the candlesticks shown actually has two spirals intertwined, a double helix, to form the decoration. A pair of the holders thus decorated will make a notable impression if set on the table before dinner. One spiraled clockwise and the other given a counterclockwise twist is most effective.

Figure 8.21. Candlesticks of wood—these of sumac—should contain metal ferrules and even then the candles should not be burned completely down.

A word of caution should be observed by anyone making and using wooden candlesticks: *Always be sure to fit the top end with a metal ferrule to protect the wood from catching fire, and as an extra precaution, do not burn the candle within an inch or two of the wood.* Thus, such pieces are recommended more as decorative additions than as a means of providing light. Even without lighting the candles, however, the candlesticks will contribute a pleasant atmosphere to a table setting.

The carving of spirals can be as simple as the design. To make a candlestick like either of those pictured, remove the bark from a straight piece 13 inches long and 1 1/4 inches in diameter, then shape the cupped end and whittle a tenon on the other to fit later into a mortise in a base of basswood or pine. Make the base 1 1/4 inches thick by 3 1/4 inches in diameter. Now lay off an 8-inch spiral on the sumac. The *lead*, that is, the vertical distance from one ridge to the next corresponding point on the same spiral, is 2 1/2 inches. This distance is twice that from ridge to adjacent ridge because there are two intertwined helixes in the item shown. A single spiral made with a 1 1/4-inch lead will have almost the same appearance as those in the photograph.

A spiral can be easily drawn by laying off the lead then drawing along the side of the tape wrapped through those points and about the piece. A felt-tip pen may be used, as in Figure 8.22, because the line will be cut away when carving. The long blade of a pocket knife or other flat blade works well. One extending across the spiral's cavity when positioned as in Figure 8.23 will help keep the spirals uniform. If desiring to carve a pair, follow the same procedure for each. The obvious difference in forming a spiral of opposite hand must be taken into account when laying out the curve with tape.

Figure 8.22. Tape wrapped about the stick is a relatively easy way to guide the drawing of a spiral

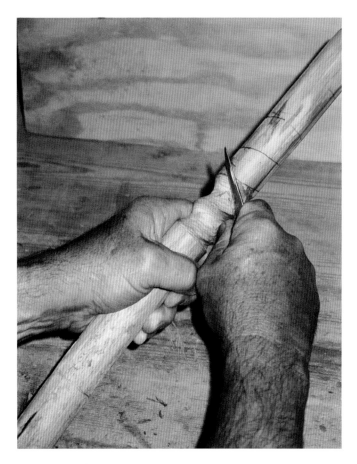

Figure 8.23. The long blade of a well-sharpened pocket knife is the tool recommended for carving spirals in a wood as soft as sumac.

Another item for challenging the designer, the final one to be covered here, can be used for cutting bread at the table or for slicing all kinds of fruit, vegetables, meat, and other foods in the kitchen. Unlike the candlesticks, which are best finished with a clear satin coating, this is the kind of item to be given occasional coats of a penetrating nontoxic substance, such as mineral oil.

Made from a solid piece of cherry wood, the 3/4 x 8 x 15 1/2-inch cutting board in Figure 8.24 has a slight taper and a carved handle for visual effect. The design at the handle covers both sides. These sparse, out-of-the-way incised details are an example of how an article of this kind can be made more interesting to view than a plain, flat board. A creative woodcarver will have no difficulty developing other designs of acceptable form.

Figure 8.24. A cutting board is another article that will challenge a person's ability to create a design for a useful product.

Chapter Nine
Ornamenting Household Furnishings

The average home contains numerous objects of practical value. In addition to the many described thus far, households are ordinarily furnished with others made of wood that could be decorated by carving. Some are fixed in place, and some are movable. Those described in this chapter pertain to furnishings commonly made part of the home environment and a few of less common use.

More Useful Applications

Practically everywhere the homeowner turns, there are places and items suitable for decorating. Lamps, pin-up boards, shelves, the fireplace mantel, stepping stools, and doorstops are among them. An entrance door made of solid wood offers another opportunity. Even the holder for our nation's flag provides an opportunity for the woodcarver to ply his or her skills.

Undoubtedly, the displaying of our flag has not often been considered a household activity, but with the recent heightened interest in placing our national symbol in view to denote solidarity of purpose and patriotism, more and more families are putting small flags on display in and about the home. That the flag is becoming a standard fixture in many households seems evident. What, therefore, could be more patriotic than to have one made part of a permanent display for visitors to see?

A small flag supported in upright position by a carving in the round seems appropriate. A carving of a person dressed in the uniform of one of the armed forces or that of a veteran's organization seems most appropriate of all. An arrangement similar to the one in Figure 9.1 is suggested. The carving has the garb of a legionnaire painted on it in applicable acrylic colors. A clear, satin polyurethane seals the painted surface.

The legionnaire stands 9 inches tall, having been carved in one piece from a block of basswood 3 inches square in cross section. A thinner piece could be used when making a figure like it by carving the projecting arm separately and attaching it. Either way, the flag bearer's attitude should be one of solemn attention. A carved piece similar to the one shown, but nearly twice as big and holding a larger flag, remains on display in a post of the American Legion.

An advantage of carving a free-standing bearer of this order is that it can be sized to suit conditions. The dimensions of the flag and the display area available are important considerations. Also, to impart the attitude intended for the design, the carving of the human figure must be properly proportioned and be realistic in all aspects of appearance. It definitely should not be a caricature.

Figure 9.1. What better way to display the national emblem than to have a carving of a serviceman, or member of a veteran's organization, hold it?

The lamp, 34 inches in height, has a cherry-wood base 5 1/2 inches square by 15 inches long. The vertical sections of 3/4-inch stock are glued together without any special joinery. The pyramid-like pieces also contain no special methods of fastening.

The carving on the base occurs on the front side only. Its form is based on a coelanaglyphic style that received prominence during ancient Egyptian times. The stylized fowl depicted has no known bearing of historic consequence. The carved features are evident in Figure 9.3. Like the many examples which have been done in stone and remained intact over the years, the design is generally flat, sharply outlined, and slightly rounded at the edges. It has minimally incised and relief-carved details. Frugality of carving seems to have been a motive compellingly driving the ancient carvers.

Figure 9.3. Details of the coelanaglyphic style of carving can be seen in this close-up of the lamp.

A Coelanaglyphic Mood

Every modern home must have a lamp. With a base of wood carved in an unusual style, the fixture can be more than just another source of light. Figure 9.2 contains an example.

Figure 9.2. The essence of an art prominently used in ancient Egypt has been captured in this modern application.

Message Bearers

Two types of message bearers are worth considering for the home. One contains slots for holding notes or letters, and the other has a cork surface for pinning papers to it. Both are useful. One, or both, may be found essential.

The first of these illustrated here (Figure 9.4) provides two open-ended slots for holding papers. It works well for holding incoming and outgoing letters. The overall dimensions of the walnut piece are 5 5/8 inches wide and 15 inches high, with a 3-inch projection of the angled parts. The back piece is 5/8 of an inch thick. The angled parts with the carved holly have a thickness of 3/8 of an inch.

Simplicity of detail, balanced arrangement, prominent placement, and naturalistic styling distinguish the sunken relief carving. At no time in the article's normal use will the decorations be completely covered, nor are they made with delicate projections which could be easily broken. The quality of the decoration, more than the article's shape and use, frequently evokes favorable comments from first-time observers.

The second type of message bearer mentioned probably provides the most preferred way of posting notes and written reminders. The large cork section of a pin-up board helps keep many such papers in view, and the pins make attaching and removing them an easy chore. An application in walnut is shown in Figure 9.5. Incised designs decorate the 10 x 22-inch piece. A simple cluster of chip-carved stars toward the top and a single line carving near the bottom are all the decorative enhancement the item needs.

Figure 9.5. The chip- and line-carved details on this walnut pin-up board are proficiently executed.

Figure 9.4. The holly carved in sunken relief on the walnut message holder shown here seems to captivate the attention of first-time viewers.

Figure 9.6. A clustered floral stylization forms the decoration on this pin-up board of cherry wood.

Where in the home should such a device be placed? A spot on the wall beside the telephone would likely be the most logical place. That is the location of the one shown in Figure 9.6. It is designed for hanging by a small finishing nail, which can scarcely be seen among the carved details near the top of the board.

This message board has details similar to the one described previously, the two being the same in size and shape. Both bear incised decorations. Only the wood used and the embellishments are different. This one has a backing of cherry wood, and as is made evident by Figure 9.7, a power tool was used to incise the decoration. The floral shapes in the design form a pattern consistent overall with the board's outline. The finished carving adds an immeasurable quality of appearance that a piece made plainly utilitarian would not generate.

Figure 9.7. The use of a power tool can simplify the carving of certain details.

Decorating Shelving

Corner shelves, straight wall shelves, and fireplace mantels are among the wooden items commonly provided in the home. They are practically indispensable for supporting and displaying both decorative and practical things. In addition to their utility, many have a decorative quality by virtue of shape and/or applied design. Ample opportunities exist for decorating by carving.

Figure 9.8 illustrates the use of a carved ornamentation on a corner shelf. Gouged and line-incised cuts form the pinecones and needles on the two surfaces. Both the shape of the assembly and details of the carved designs bear scrutiny.

Figure 9.8. A light stain has brought out the gouged and line-incised design on this pine shelf.

The shelf is pine of 3/8-inch thickness. It is 10 inches high and projects 5 3/4 inches from the corner along each wall. The light stain covering the assembly helps bring out the carved features.

The carving of pierced wood is another way to decorate shelves, particularly if made with brackets. An application appears in Figure 9.9. The material is cherry wood of 3/8-inch thickness, having overall dimensions as assembled of 5 x 5 1/2 x 14 inches. Three spots are carved: the two brackets and the bottom edge of the central strip. The brackets are carved in relief, and the central piece is embellished slightly by edge carving—a way of designing and carving described later in Chapter 13. None of the carvings, it is important to note, seriously impair the strength of the member to which they are applied.

Figure 9.9. Designs pierced and carved on a shelf's brackets are preferably shaped front and back in bold relief.

The brackets on the shelf contain a stylized arrangement of flowers and leaves in bold relief. When making a decoration of this type, piercing must precede the carving. A scroll saw can be used, as in Figure 9.10, to remove the parts of wood to be discarded. Both sides of the cutout must then be shaped to form the obverse and reverse surfaces of the figures. The finished brackets are assembled so that the front side of each design faces outward.

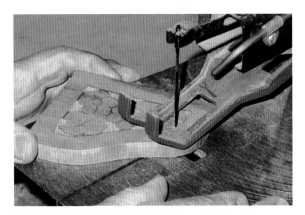

Figure 9.10. The removal of wood where not wanted in a pierced design is best achieved by using a scroll saw before carving the shapes.

Homes are often designed with a fireplace which has a mantel over it. The mantels are often used as shelves, and some are decorated by carving. As with shelves generally, a design on a structure over a fireplace opening should be such that the details cannot be easily damaged when placing and removing items of display.

A mantel carved by an expert relief carver is shown in Figure 9.11. It is accompanied by a close-up of his boldly carved oak leaves and acorns in Figure 9.12. The skillful detailing of features in natural form and the effective stippling of wood in the background are apparent in the photographs. However, the delicacy of the leaves and twigs represented would seem to warrant some caution by anyone standing or working in the vicinity. The woodcarver, to his credit, has provided a considerable amount of protection by having recessed the carved details. The projecting border of solid wood undoubtedly helps protect against damage. Without it, a carving of that kind would be totally out of place on a mantel or on any other kind of shelf. The quality and beauty of the piece shown makes an excellent study for anyone interested in naturalistic carving in bold relief.

Figure 9.11. This beautiful fireplace mantel, which also serves as a shelf, has a projecting wood border to help protect the boldly carved decoration.

Figure 9.12. This close-up, showing the delicately shaped oak leaves, twigs, and acorns, reveals the woodcarver's skill in duplicating nature.

For Stepping Up

Have you ever wanted to give someone a gift for which you will be long remembered? If the person in mind is a housewife, present a handcrafted stepping stool to her. She will probably thank you and think of you often for having placed one in her possession, for few women can get by without some assistance when reaching the top shelves in the kitchen. Although you could make an impression with a stool of ordinary form, consider making the gift truly special by hand carving a design on its sides.

A leaf-and-flower design seems suitable. One such may be seen in Figure 9.13. In this application, the design is carved in relief on an area to the piece's side where it will not be subject to damage due to wear. A similar carving decorates the surface on the opposite side of the pine stool. The design, 2 3/4 inches wide by 8 inches long, is shown in Figure 9.14 as cut into a cardboard template for outlining the shape. Depth about the outline is achieved by gouging the soft wood with a small handheld tool (Figure 9.15). Touch-up sanding of the finished work can be done conveniently using a stiff emery board, as in Figure 9.16.

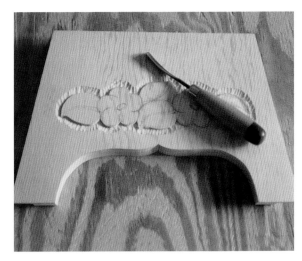

Figure 9.15. A small handheld gouge will be adequate for producing depth around a design in soft pine.

Figure 9.13. A stepping stool—this sturdy one made for one-hand lifting—can be adequately embellished with a design in relief on opposite sides.

Figure 9.16. An emery board is useful for touching up a carving of this kind before assembling the article's parts.

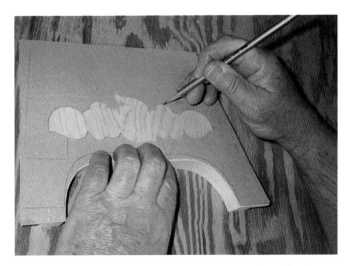

Figure 9.14. Cardboard cut from a cereal box makes a good template for outlining a design on multiple pieces.

Anyone planning to make a stepping stool is advised to observe the features incorporated in the design presented here. First of all, utility takes precedence over esthetics in an application of this kind. No decoration, no matter how beautiful, will compensate for a stool that doesn't serve its purpose well. One made too low can cause almost as much of a problem as one requiring the person to step too high. A 9 1/2-inch height will prove adequate for general use.

Secondly, sturdiness and stability are important. The person using the stool must feel safely supported. A top piece made about 1 1/8 of an inch thick, 9 1/2 inches wide, and 12 inches long will have the size and substantiality desired. Sidepieces of 3/4 of an inch thickness are entirely adequate as positioned. Additionally, the sides are best flared on a 10-degree angle. Not only does this allow for spreading the stool's feet to a point nearly in line with the top's perimeter, thereby, increasing stability over that possible with vertical sides, but also it presents surfaces for decorating which are more readily viewed from above.

Convenience and comfort are the remaining considerations of importance relative to a stool's utility. A slot properly shaped and centered in the top piece serves an important purpose. This little feature enables a user to lift and move a stool about comfortably with one hand, leaving the other free to do other work. Moreover, the user should feel comfortable handling the piece. The decorative details, particularly, must not be made so sharp and delicate that the user will feel ill at ease for fear of damaging some part.

The decorating of a foot stool raises another point of concern. Placement is the issue. The design might be good, the carved features might have adequate form and smoothness, and the craftsmanship could be superb in quality, yet virtually all would go for naught if poorly placed. Ruling out the top surface where stepping would wear away any decoration placed there, the place for adornment is somewhere along the side. But where? Where the carved details will be visible to persons standing. That spot on a stool with angled sides is toward the cutout edge near the bottom on each large side. Whether this spot will be above, on, or below the mid-height of the side does not matter much. The important requirement is to avoid, to a permissible extent, hiding the carving beneath the overhang. The decoration should be fully evident under most normal conditions of viewing from above.

A design slightly different from that in the previous example is shown in Figure 9.17. It, and the fir stool it decorates, meets the requirements deemed important, but in this case, the design stands out more prominently by virtue of the wood having been given an application of oil stain. Designs may also be incised on stepping stools. A design for incising is included in Figure 9.18.

Figure 9.17. This stained fir stool is similar in design to the one shown previously, except for differences in the floral decorations.

Figure 9.18. Patterns for decorating stepping stools may be designed for incising as well as for carving in relief.

Door Stopping

The ready availability of commercially manufactured devices for keeping doors in the home from slamming on breezy summer days indicates how commonly doorstops are being used today. Many of the wedge-shaped devices are strictly utilitarian. Esthetic value does not generally exist. The opportunity for creating desirable pieces in wood that are both useful and decorative seems obvious.

Door stops of wood have two essential parts: The front piece may be of a figure carved in some degree of roundness, with a second piece in the shape of a wedge attached to it. The wedge, made with a taper from a block of wood 1 1/8 x 2 1/2 x 3 inches, is the utilitarian part which wedges under a door to stop it from swinging. This piece attaches to the larger, more decorative piece along its bottom edge by means of glue and dowel pins.

The decorative piece, sometimes made of wood 1 1/2 x 7 1/2 x 10 inches in size, may be carved on its outer face in shallow detail. The carving may vary from the precisely realistic to a totally abstract form of representation. Stylized shapes are permissible, and their use can create a bit of humor. A novel creation of a modified naturalistic style is shown being traced in Figure 9.19. This one might be designated "a protective puppy," but other representations would do just as well. A design created in the likeness of a favorite pet might be a more meaningful representation for some families.

Figure 9.19. A drawing of a pet in stylized form is shown being traced onto 1 1/2-inch fir for constructing a doorstop.

The carving of the front and manner of attaching the door wedge to the flat back of the upright piece are shown in Figures 9.20 and 9.21. The wedge was glued in place after all carving on the front had been completed. Selected from pieces prepared for house construction, the soft fir wood used to form the puppy displayed the variation in color desired. The wedge was cut from a pine board. The two pieces were ultimately assembled, stained, and sparingly painted. Acrylic paints were used for emphasizing a few selected features, as in Figure 9.22. When dry, the entire item was sealed with a spray of non-glossy polyurethane. Figure 9.23 shows the result.

Figure 9.22. Stain and a few painted spots bring out the carved features of the finished doorstop.

Figure 9.20. The contour of the doorstop is carved on one side of the piece in shallow, partly round detail.

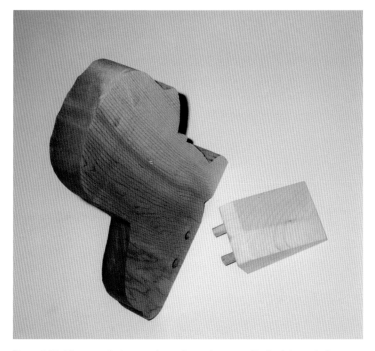

Figure 9.21. The carved piece works well as a doorstop if its back is made for attaching a wedge low in slope.

Figure 9.23. This finished figure indicates a designer has a wide latitude of options to call on when fashioning doorstops.

As suggested, naturalistic forms can be modified or have certain features distorted to create the kind of impression desired. An occasional display of a human characteristic in the portrayal of an animal can get across a point impressively. All sorts of moods can be displayed. Persons who want a humorous effect, for example, might consider one of the figures outlined in the accompanying sketches (Figures 9.24 and 9.25). They are novel creations, certainly, but they are indicative of how animal forms might be styled for use on practical applications of this kind. A young, fun-loving member of the home just might relish having one of those critters propping the door open in his or her bedroom.

D a p p e r

D u c k

Figure 9.24. A doorstop designed with a humorous flair might be just the thing needed for holding a door open on a warm, windy day.

P e t i e

L a P e w

DON'T PUSH IT !!

Figure 9.25. A fun-loving member of the house would likely relish having a stop for his or her bedroom door fashioned in the form of this critter.

Door Adornment

The front door of a home offers another opportunity for displaying one's skill in woodcarving. The door must be solid wood or, at the very least, have a panel of solid wood. One in which the craftsman first decorated a panel and then had the door's stiles and rails built about it is shown in Figure 9.26. The wood is walnut. It has the special qualities desired for receiving and displaying a unique decoration. The creator of the piece is the same craftsman who carved the fireplace mantel shown earlier.

Figure 9.26. Assembled after all carving was completed, this walnut door contains a relief carving neatly done in realistic style.

The naturalistic scene has been carved in relief. The cleverly arranged details can only be fully appreciated by seeing what each section holds. As may be apparent in the close-up of the panel (Figure 9.27), the owl appears to be descending on a partly hidden rodent in the leaves below and to the lower-left side. Only the head of the wary mouse appears from beneath the leaves depicted in the small carving. By carving in sunken relief, as was done in this application, the surrounding surface effectively aids in protecting the tooled design.

Figure 9.27. The precision in this clever arrangement (a mouse peeks from under leaves in the lower left cell) is evident in the details.

How the woodcarver tied in representations of nature by overlapping a bit of the flat surface along the scene's edge is worth noting, for it is a technique that avoids the monotony of a plane, unbroken edge throughout. Other features deserve attention, too. The textured tree trunk, the realistically shaped leaves, and the stippled background are among them. These may be seen in the close-up of the work done while in progress (Figure 9.28). It is definitely the work of a skillful relief carver.

Figure 9.28. The woodcarver's proficient use of stippling can be seen in the close-up of the carving in progress.

Chapter Ten
Embellishing Turned Articles

The primary reason for carving articles shaped on a wood-turning lathe is decoration. Carved areas on turned articles that are easily moved about by hand do sometimes serve a minor utilitarian purpose. That could occur, as explained before for other applications, if the object is grasped about the carved decoration. This possibility, even if it should occur as suggested, is comparatively insignificant in importance. The decorative quality of the carving is the primary concern in constructing most turned articles. An important matter to consider when creating the design is the purpose of creating a carving that will be durable and comfortable to the touch.

The Procedure

When preparing wood for turning that will also be carved, knowledge of carving becomes as important as knowledge of construction. An area to be decorated generally requires treatment during the turning process according to the method of decorating. An article to be relief carved may require that an elevated ridge be provided about its circumference, but for incising the same region, only a relatively plain surface may be needed. In a real sense, carving and turning are integrated.

This relationship holds true for faceplate work and for objects turned between centers. The main difference of concern to the woodcarver is the direction of the wood's grain. Objects turned between centers generally have the grain positioned lengthwise, thereby, presenting easily carved side grain about the article's entire exterior surface. Faceplate turnings, on the other hand, are often made from blocks of wood such that both end grain and side grain will appear on an article's circumference. Bowls are usually faceplate turnings. The woodcarver will take their varied grain structure into consideration when carving a design about the item's perimeter.

Other points to consider are a design's layout and manner of carving. Designs can often be drawn directly on a product while still mounted in the lathe. This practice is shown being applied to the faceplate turning of a bowl (Figure 10.1). On occasion, the carving of details can then proceed directly in the lathe. There are times, too, when the piece must be moved to another location for carving.

As to manner of carving, the depth of carving, the firmness of the wood, and the thickness of the material in the finished container are important. All enter into the determination of whether to carve an article's surface before or after removing wood from its inside. Weak woods, members to be made very thin about the perimeter, and carving requiring the force of a mallet are potential

Figure 10.1. If it is to be carved, a bowl turned on the lathe's faceplate must be provided with an edge thick enough to accommodate the decoration.

indicators that the carving should be done before removing wood from the internal section. The solid backup of the central core may be necessary. By the same token, any carving done prior to removing the container's core must be adequately protected against damage when completing the construction.

Relief Applications

Designs on turned articles are very often carved in strip form, with a series of figures repeated about the object's circumference. On cylindrical objects, as is true for many other useful pieces, figures in relief are often based on some form of plant life. Figure 10.2 contains an example. A line of similar flower heads makes up the weed pot's design. They project approximately 3/16 of an inch and have a 1-inch diameter. The thin, non-glossy finish covering the pot consists entirely of two coats of satin polyurethane.

Figure 10.2. Both the carved weed pot and its dried contents vie for attention in this display.

Turned from a piece of 4 x 4 redwood held between centers on the lathe, the finished dimensions of the weed pot are 3 1/4 inches in diameter near the bottom and 7 inches in height. A 1 1/4-inch hole bored 4 inches deep accommodates the stems of a small bunch of weeds. Sprigs of dry pampas grass, cattails, teasel, pussy willow buds, and eucalyptus can be intermixed and arranged for display. A light application of hair spray on the weeds helps keep them from deteriorating rapidly.

The redwood serves its purpose satisfactorily, but when considered from the standpoint of carving, it proves to be adequate only because the details do not require a great deal of precision. Nevertheless, commendable results are obtainable by using sharp tools and exercising care in offsetting the soft, grainy wood's tendency to splinter and chip.

The process of decorating begins with the stock in the lathe. The wood turner leaves a section stand for the relief carving (Figure 10.3), with the size and location of this projection depending on the carving to be accommodated. Obviously, details of the design must be established beforehand for this to be done accurately. The turning is eventually removed from the lathe for the boring of the hole.

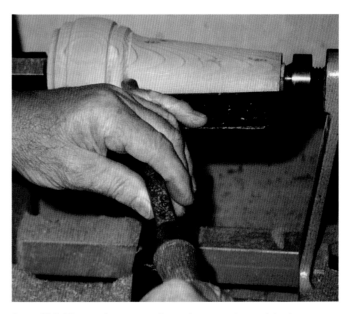

Figure 10.3. The woodcarver must know the eventual size of the design in order to leave a ridge elevated as needed for the relief carving.

After the preparatory operations have been completed, the elevated section can be divided to receive the carving. A strip of paper serves the purpose. There may be no better way to obtain the weed pot's exact circumference in the area to be carved than by wrapping a long strip of paper about the object. The method has a further advantage in that the measurement taken will be immediately available and in convenient form for marking off equal steps for the decorative details. The strip shown in Figure 10.4 contains evenly sized spaces. With the strip wrapped about the pot's largest circumference, comparable spaces are marked on the wood to guide the sketching of each flower.

Some adjustment in design will often be necessary when determining the number of units making up a pattern about a turned surface. One hopes in the process to obtain the number

Figure 10.4. A strip of paper is very useful for determining a circumference and dividing it to accommodate equal units of design.

of divisions needed for sizing all units exactly as intended. That seldom happens. For example, in a design where the units are to be, say, 3/4 of an inch square, the units may have to be made slightly rectangular or have their height adjusted to equal the horizontal dimension found to be nearest the measurement desired. The difficulty posed by this example commonly occurs when decorating cylindrical work, but in all probability, such an occurrence will not be sufficient reason for scrapping the design and starting over. How many people will notice a problem with a design in which each unit has had to be made a tiny fraction of an inch smaller or larger than the designer initially intended?

Although not everyone will agree, the carving of the weed pot just might be the most enjoyable part of the entire process. With each flower sketched in place, the shaping proceeds by incising about the penciled outlines. The next step involves paring away the wood in surrounding areas. A flat blade can be used to do this, as in Figure 10.5. The knife is also useful for rounding parts and separating petals.

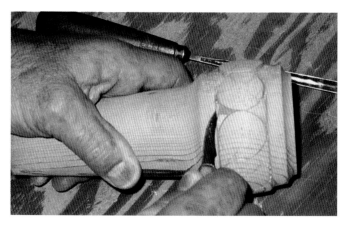

Figure 10.5. Carving knives are used to incise outlines, whittle away background wood, and pare the centers of the flowers.

Gouging adds the detail desired within each flower (Figure 10. 6). It is coordinated with knife work in the carving operation, which completes the item except for applying a finish.

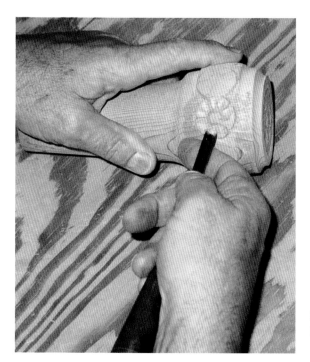

Figure 10.6. Gouges are used intermittently with carving knives to produce the depth and detail desired.

Another carved article—this one done in a more naturalistic form of relief—may be seen in Figure 10.7. The shallow bowl contains an undulating vine-and-leaf decoration. The bowl is pine, 1 3/4 inches high by 9 3/8 inches in diameter. It functions effectively for holding pretzels or other snack foods. The beginner who created the piece deserves credit for the rhythmically undulating carving, although the leaves might have been modified for the sake of appearance and to present shapes more comfortable for holding and carrying. Perhaps, this example will stimulate others to step into the challenging arena of designing and carving bowls.

Figure 10.7. This relief-carved bowl, while having a basically meritorious design, could be improved by reshaping the design's leaves.

Plane-Relief Decorations

As with other forms of relief carving, plane carving necessitates recessing the wood surrounding the figures in a design, but unlike relief carving generally, the tops of figures remain in the plane of the wood's surface. Plane relief will often be used to produce bold lettering and to decorate articles that can only take shallow carving. Although the depth of carving may vary from application to application, the depth in some items does not exceed 3/32 of an inch. The texturing of wood then becomes virtually essential to accentuate the contrast between the figures and surrounding areas. Stippling is a frequently used technique for doing that.

The design on the weed pot of mahogany included in Figure 10.8 has been carved in plane relief. Plant-like shapes were chosen for the design because of their apparent relationship to the article's use. The spot chosen for the carved strip was simply to place the decoration where, due to considerations of size, it would have considerable visual impact. The taller redwood vessel was treated similarly, except that the decorative pattern was incised.

Figure 10.9. The decoration on this paper clip tray is another example of a useful project being embellished with a design carved in plane relief.

Figure 10.8. One carved in plane relief and the other chip-carved, these two weed pots are examples of ways to shape and decorate such articles.

The berry-and-leaf pattern decorating the paper-clip container (Figure 10.9) is another example of plane relief. The article, being only 2 1/2 inches high by 3 inches in diameter, has a ribbon design in which individual units repeat nearly every 1 3/32 inches about the article's circumference. Stippled areas surround the shapes. The stippling process is shown in Figure 10.10. It helps make the finished details stand out, after staining the item. Once again, the design does not duplicate reality, nor has there been any attempt to have it do so. Nevertheless, the outlined shapes with their plane surfaces are strongly suggestive of natural three-dimensional form.

Figure 10.10. The stippling of surrounding wood gives the outlined details prominence in a carving done in plane relief.

The acceptance of plane-relief carving as a decorative art stems somewhat from our familiarity with drawn and printed art. Three-dimensional forms are commonly represented in two dimensions in such work. Examples are all around us. Designs on wallpaper, paintings on billboards, drawings in books, illustrations in magazines, and so forth, indicate the numerous uses of flat representation to depict objects in the round. Who among us has not viewed and come to accept this two-dimensional form of representation? Plane carving capitalizes on our experience with flat illustration, but it then goes one step beyond. It moves closer to reality by producing shapes which are partly three-dimensional.

Although plant life is a primary source of inspiration for designing in relief, considerable latitude exists for using designs of other types. Animals are a good source. While the possibilities are theoretically without restriction, the woodcarver should consider the advantage in portraying a friendly household pet in certain decorations. A series of dogs or cats, as in Figure 10.11, could be a good starting point. Not to be overlooked, certainly, are the interests of youngsters who prefer things a bit more ghoulish than that. Something slightly weird or dragon-like may actually be preferred by a teenager.

Figure 10.11. Youngsters might not be the only people who occasionally want their projects decorated with animals in some form.

Incised Designs

Articles turned in a lathe can often be completed more readily when they are to be incised, rather than carved in relief. One reason is that an article can be shaped without building in a raised portion. Avoiding this step enables the designer to proceed without accommodating the specific features of the decoration to be used. In other words, an incised decoration's size and placement on an object's perimeter might not have to be precisely determined and provided for ahead of the shaping operation. Seeing the object in the round beforehand could also work to the woodcarver's advantage on occasion, although having the entire design on hand, complete with decoration, remains the practice to be preferred.

Several examples are included in this section. The first (Figure 10.12) is a walnut pencil holder with a spot design that has

been incised with knife and gouges of different sizes. The holder's outside diameter is 3 1/4 inches and its height, 4 inches. The grain runs lengthwise, a condition favorable for hand carving anywhere about the outside surface. The subject of the carving seems to interest boys and girls of school age most of all.

Figure 10.12. A pencil holder with stylized flowers and bees incised on it will likely invite a bit of conversation from observers.

The second incised piece to be discussed has been completed in a different manner (Figure 10.13). The pine bowl was first turned on a faceplate from a block 2 3/4 inches thick by 9 inches in diameter. The continuous detail about its circumference was then made with a power-driven rotary burr, an initial effort by a student to do the incising completely using a power tool. To the student's credit, the design was incised with only enough detail to add interest without detracting radically from the bowl and its purpose. The decorating was done in an appropriate location, as well. In this case, as in all others involving designs of discernible significance, the question remains as to whether the quality of the carving measures up to that of the design.

Figure 10.13. This pine bowl, with its clean, simple design, is a first effort to incise the design entirely by power carving with a rotary bit.

Figure 10.15. Some projects can be most easily held in position for drawing and carving the design while the piece remains in the lathe.

The next item illustrated has been given an incised decoration of still another kind (Figure 10.14). This small candy dish was decorated after turning a block of pine 1 1/2 inches by 5 1/2 inches diameter and then band sawing away two sides to a distance 4 1/2 inches across. The next step involved drawing the design in preparation for incising the flat surfaces remaining on opposite ends. The drawing, as in Figure 10.15, and the carving occurred with the dish securely held in the lathe.

The fourth, and final, item to be presented in this section for purposes of showing the extensive variety of designs possible by incising is a cylindrical bank. The construction of this article is no different from that explained in the chapter on coin banks; it simply presents another option of use in the decorating of turned objects. Hearts, high and low, give the bank a homey appearance. The hand-carved features are large enough so that the paint did not obliterate any of the details (Figure 10.16). Both the colors and the design have qualities known to be favored by the person for whom the bank was made. Such knowledge can be extremely helpful when creating a design.

Figure 10.14. As shown in this application, a tray turned on a lathe need not always be decorated by carving along a vertical side.

Figure 10.16. Still another design for incising can be seen in this use of hearts on a turned coin bank.

Chip-Carved Variations

Chip carving has emerged as a specialized form of incising. The designs possible by the method are virtually limitless. They may be applied to cylindrical shapes in one of two ways: by spreading the designs over broad areas or by connecting the details in ribbon-like circumferential strips.

One chip carving covering much of the surface on the lid of a jewelry box is shown in Figure 10.17. The pattern on the curved top follows the surface's outline in a general way, and it is composed of a variety of interwoven circular elements. These features create a compatible appearance between the box and its design. The angle of lighting used to produce the picture emphasizes the depth of tooling involved. It also indicates somewhat the thickness of material used at that point to accommodate the tooling. The basswood box's overall dimensions are 3 3/4 inches by 4 inches diameter.

Figure 10.17. Chip-carved designs, being basically geometric, challenge the designer to produce interlaced details that are variable and fitting.

As might be expected, a compass becomes essential for drawing patterns radiating in circular fashion from a central point (Figure 10.18). The development of details on paper continues to be the recommendation for applications of this kind, although the final design can be most conveniently drawn directly on the surface to be carved. Chip carving, properly done, will remove the lines formed by the instrument's lead point. This holds true even for lines drawn to indicate the high points of the design, if they have not been deeply gouged into the wood by applying too much pressure on the compass.

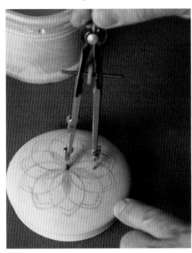

Figure 10.18. A compass is essential when drawing circular patterns for chip carving cylindrical objects.

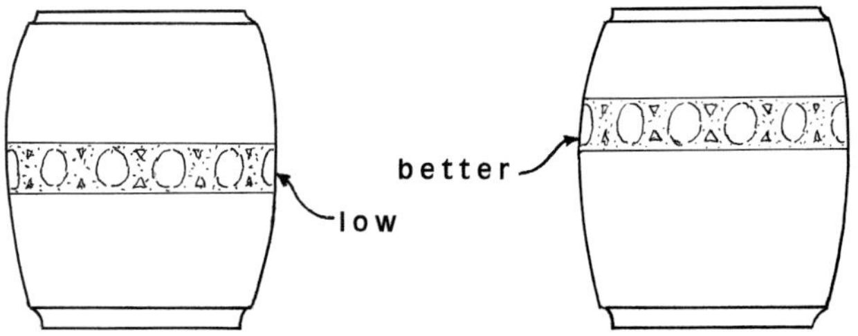

The second type of chip-carved design, the strip pattern, also can be applied in any of the many geometric arrangements possible. An application on a pen holder is shown in Figure 10.19. The strip's size, location, and simplicity are its strong features. The fir holder has a 2 1/2-inch height and a 3 3/4-inch diameter. One such article could be decorated with a larger, more elaborate circumferential pattern and still have acceptable qualities, but the concern for placing the strip at the best height on the most visible surface would remain as before. A recommendation on this matter is given in Figure 10.20. It applies to the positioning of decorative strips on vertical surfaces, regardless of the method of carving.

Figure 10.19. A pen holder is another desk accessory suitable for carving in repetitive, ribbon-like sequence to embellish a plain area.

Figure 10.20. The placement of a design on a vertical surface requires a critical eye if it is to be optically pleasing.

The recommendation in the drawing is not the only concern, however. A carved strip's size and its distance to the nearest edge are other points bearing emphasis. Briefly, the distance from the edge of a strip to the nearest edge of the item should be made more or less than the strip's vertical dimension, i.e., its width. The idea is to avoid the monotonous appearance created by a series of equally spaced straight lines. There are no precise measurements to be followed. The designer's judgment and sense of what will be esthetically pleasing are the essential guides in this matter.

Texture and Color

Articles made for practical use can be enhanced by techniques other than those previously shown. These additional techniques are very simple. One involves the use of texture created by tooling, and the other makes use of acrylic paint to bring out details.

Texturing, as used on the candlesticks in Figure 10.21, is simply a matter of tooling a surface in a manner usually reserved for the background areas in relief carving. Gouging in a random pattern is preferred. It effectively alters a surface and counterbalances smoothness in other areas of a product. Properly done, texturing provides all the decorating an item needs. Notice, in the illustration, how the carving seems to reinforce the design rather than dominate or detract from the impact provided by the candlesticks' lines. This application shows how subtle a carved design can be and still be impressive.

Figure 10.21. Texturing a surface by means of a method usually reserved for carving background areas in relief is all that some surfaces need.

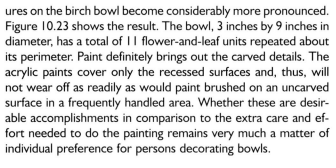

ures on the birch bowl become considerably more pronounced. Figure 10.23 shows the result. The bowl, 3 inches by 9 inches in diameter, has a total of 11 flower-and-leaf units repeated about its perimeter. Paint definitely brings out the carved details. The acrylic paints cover only the recessed surfaces and, thus, will not wear off as readily as would paint brushed on an uncarved surface in a frequently handled area. Whether these are desirable accomplishments in comparison to the extra care and effort needed to do the painting remains very much a matter of individual preference for persons decorating bowls.

Figure 10.22. A bowl that has end grain in areas about its circumference can be decorated most easily by incising with a power tool.

Think of other possible uses for a textured pattern. Look at some of the examples previously shown. Could, for instance, the chip-carved design on the pen holder in Figure 10.19 be replaced with a uniformly textured pattern? It could be, certainly, and you just might prefer it that way.

Color is another way to enhance woodcarvings, but its use is not new. Carvings in the round are frequently painted, and relief carvings, as well as some chip-carved patterns, are sometimes stained. The reasons are to provide a realistic appearance or to emphasize certain details. Less common is the use of acrylic paint on decorative strips that have been incised.

The use of colorful paints in the cavities of carved details may be most preferred when the decoration lacks the prominence necessary to be noticed in ordinary situations. The strip shown being incised with a power carver in Figure 10.22 illustrates the type. When painted with vivid colors, the incised fig-

Figure 10.23. While painting incised details with acrylic colors takes time and care, there are those who contend the result is worth the effort.

Color and texture, as with some of the other applications shown here, offer the curious woodcarver alternatives to customarily practiced types of decorating. Whether they are or are not advocated by the author is not the point of importance. Knowing they are available for application to a variety of useful products is important for the complete development of the designer-craftsman.

Chapter Eleven
Making Distinctive Walking Sticks

Walking sticks, by definition, are comprised of canes and long, generally straight staffs. Both can assist when walking, with canes often being essential for that purpose. For convenience in distinguishing between the two, hereafter the term "walking sticks" will denote shafts of wood made for hiking or strolling, and "canes" will be reserved for the shorter devices that contain a handle to lean on for support.

The bark of the branches and saplings used in constructing the two forms may either be left intact or be removed. Modification by carving is possible in either case. Methods of carving in the round, several variations of relief carving, and incising are applicable.

Design Styles

Designs carved on walking sticks are primarily decorative, but some also serve a practical purpose. The difference occurs as a consequence of location. A section carved on a staff at the point of gripping while walking will aid in holding the piece, while one positioned above or below that spot will be solely decorative. Experienced hikers know that some configuration or roughness is needed on a stick for comfort and ease in gripping. The texture of natural bark will often be sufficient. If too smooth, however, the hand must be clamped evermore tightly to prevent slippage when walking. The woodcarver can help avoid the problem by placing the decoration in the appropriate area. A loop of leather might also be attached to a stick where it will serve as a handhold.

Carvings in the round on walking sticks are almost always decorative. One such terminates the upper end of the stick shown in Figure 11.1. It is there for viewing, not holding. The line-incised section, the section below the carved owl, covers the area of gripping and provides the configuration needed by a walker. The curvature of the stick at that point also assists, for the reason that the crease formed by the hand when clenched and extended straight forward does not form a vertical line but one angled slightly forward at the top. This provision, while not entirely essential, enables the walker to carry the stick more to the vertical than conveniently possible with a straight staff.

Figure 11.1. While the decorative carving attached to the top of this walking stick will surely gain attention, the curved area will assist in gripping.

Decorate a walking stick in the manner shown and you might find that some observers will comment favorably about the piece. Carry it in a park where many others walk and you can be virtually certain of special attention. Somebody might even inquire about buying the piece.

Any carved figure attached to the top of a waking stick functions not only as an enhancement and an inducement for conversation, but also as a possible means of gaining new acquaintances. The stick, itself, provides significant benefits. Its assistance while walking up an incline, its use in pushing aside brush along a hiking trail, and the peace of mind it produces as an instrument of personal protection are likely to be appreciated most of all.

A walking stick of a style in which the decorated area falls at the point of gripping is shown in Figure 11.2. The flowers are carved in relief. Their smoothly configured form and amount of projection contribute to the utilitarian value of the design without causing discomfort to the hand. The curvature of the stick, as previously explained, is another plus for the design. Only selected areas are covered with acrylic paint, but polyurethane protects both the painted and unpainted surfaces. The position of the carving for convenience in holding is about 38 to 44 inches from the carving's center to the stick's bottom tip, a distance suitable for a woman of average height. About 4 inches must be added to those dimensions for most men.

Figure 11.2. A design in relief, when carved on a curved section at the point of holding, creates a very effective handgrip on a walking stick.

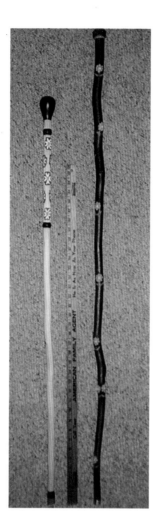

Figure 11.3. Walking sticks may be made in various lengths and designs, but each should have the tip at the bottom protected against excessive wear

Figure 11.4. Areas plane carved by removing sections of bark make attractive designs on walking sticks when painted in bold colors.

As with any stick intended for use when walking, including the pair shown in Figure 11.3, the bottom end must be provided with some device for preventing excessive wear. A rubber cup or metal sleeve covering the tip and a wood screw inserted into the end with head exposed are among the solutions possible. Each method seems to offer as many advantages and disadvantages as the next.

Relief carving of a slightly different type decorates the walking sticks in Figure 11.4. It is bark carving, a variety of plane relief. In this application, the bark still covers the sticks, except in parts of the designs creating the patterns. Color adds to their attractiveness. The wood exposed, where sections of bark were removed, is left unpainted. Whether or not the patterns fall on or above the spot of holding does not really matter, because the natural texture of the bark covering the shafts will sufficiently aid in gripping when walking. Both sticks have the tightly attached bark characteristic of the poplar saplings from which they were cut.

The next method of carving to be illustrated is incising. Decorative chip-carved patterns, line carvings, and gouged forms are applicable to the decorating of walking sticks, and either knives or power tools may be used as found most convenient. A pattern created by chip carving with flat blades is shown in Figure 11.5. The simply incised design is entirely decorative, being below the leather strap made for holding and on opposite sides of the oak shaft. This example shows that, in addition to the inherent quality of simple design, the material for making walking sticks need not always be taken directly from the forest.

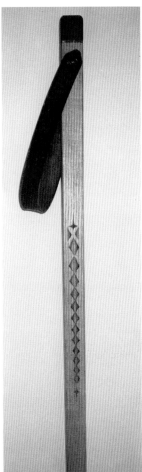

Figure 11.5. Incising, whether done by chip carving as in this example or in another form, can be very impressive when efficaciously applied.

Functional Accommodations

There are several important matters regarding esthetics and utility still to be considered in the design of a walking stick. Matters of straightness, balance, strength, handgrip, and tip-design particularly bear further explanation. How they are taken into account during construction will affect functionality. To put in time carving a stick that will not measure up practically makes little sense.

First of all, the piece must be long enough and strong enough for the purpose. Most saplings and young branches will do if not excessively dry, rotting, split, or checked, but a weak wood, such as cottonwood, will probably not provide the strength desired even if it does not contain noticeable defects. Knots are another concern. Sticks that are weak because of a loose knot or two should be discarded.

Sticks with firmly attached knots are another matter, entirely. Carving them is seldom the problem. A woodcarver's tools must be sharp enough to cut through such growth. The problem may be one of appearance. Too many knots could detract

from the design. Applications of paint to match them to the surrounding surface will sometimes hide the blemishes sufficiently. Be aware, on the other hand, that the presence of knots is often desired in rustic applications.

Sticks that are bowed or have unsightly bends can often be made usable by straightening. Sharp kinks cannot be easily eliminated, and their presence does preserve the natural effect, but the more general curves and bends that make a stick appear out of balance or distorted should be corrected. Fortunately, there is a way to treat such problems so that a staff's form will follow a generally straight line from end to end.

The process of straightening begins with steaming. This operation may be done on the kitchen range (with permission granted by the lady of the house, of course) by boiling water in a pan to soften the area of curvature. As in Figure 11.6, a cloth covering the stick and pan will contain the steam. How long to steam a stick depends on its thickness and species, although, roughly speaking, five to ten minutes will be adequate for pieces of an inch to 1 1/2 inches in diameter. Whether a stick has been shaved bare or remains covered with bark matters little. Even previously finished pieces can be steamed without seriously affecting the work.

Figure 11.6. The process of removing an undesirable bend from a stick begins with steaming, as is being done by boiling water on a kitchen range.

When a bent section has become sufficiently pliable, the stick should be removed from the heat and be promptly straightened by flexing it in a direction opposite the bend. Flexing can be done several ways. One way is over a knee, and another requires standing on the stick's one end and lifting the other to the extent that, upon relaxing this pressure, the staff will return to a straight line but not its original bend. Care is necessary to avoid cracking or splitting the wood by over-bending. Steaming and flexing can be done repeatedly. Large bends and initial efforts could, and often do, require several such attempts. Once straightened and dry, a stick will retain its new shape permanently.

With a stick of adequate size and shape in hand, questions relative to decorative design, the handgrip, and treatment of the bottom section often remain to be answered. As to kind and style of decoration, the designs in this chapter provide ideas in sufficient quantity for aspiring beginners and experienced woodcarvers to proceed on their own. The options for dealing with the other concerns mentioned are less dependent on knowledge of what will serve best esthetically. For example, what form of handgrip would be effective on a walking stick that has no natural bend to hold onto, especially if too thin for an incised pattern of intersecting lines to do much good, and cannot be provided with another carved area or a leather loop because a carving in the round has been attached to the stick's upper end? None of the methods previously suggested will do. An application subject to the conditions mentioned is shown in Figure 11.7. The braided leather piece surrounding the stick at the spot of gripping provides the solution. A wooden grip in the form of a torus would also work in conjunction with the naturally grown, spiraled shape attached to the staff. While the stick's design is unique, the potential for using a handgrip as shown is far reaching.

Figure 11.7. A naturally grown spiral, with an automotive body filler shaped and carved to form the head, tops this one-of-a-kind walking stick.

What about the treatment of the foot-end of a walking stick? Some means of covering the tip is desirable. The unprotected bottom end of a walking stick will wear away through normal use. Several solutions are available. One is to fit a rubber cup on the tip. These devices are sold commercially for covering the ends of canes, but cups of the sizes needed for sticks of various diameters are not always available. Another solution entails dipping the tip of the stick in liquid plastic, which, when dry, forms a shield much like a rubber cup. Plastic dip forms a commendably tight fit. Unfortunately, it lacks the durability needed to hold up under extensive use.

A third solution involves fitting a piece of metal pipe on the stick's end. Numerous sizes of pipe are obtainable, but a bit of whittling of the stick will usually be required for a perfect fit. A metal sleeve will not fall off if tightly fit and slightly crimped at its

inner end. One made of copper tubing covers the tip of the walking stick shown in Figure 11.8. Copper holds up reasonably well, and it does not rust. It tarnishes. An occasional cleaning with steel wool and coating with a protective finish will help maintain a bright sheen. Despite their benefits, metal tips have, at least, potentially another disadvantage. Frequent use will result in a burr being formed where the metal tip strikes the ground. This could be most damaging if a stick so equipped is stored inside on a carpeted floor.

Figure 11.8. A piece of copper tubing to protect this walking stick's tip and a ring carved near the end for adding color are important additions.

In the accompanying photograph, a knife is shown in use for forming a ring near the end of the stick. Placed there for reasons of esthetics, the ring will be carved and painted to complement the decoration on a stick's other end. Such rings need not be large, but they are desirable embellishments. In this instance, the ring serves a special purpose. Its placement is such that the brushing of an opaque acrylic paint between the carved lines will also cover an unsightly knot.

Three-Dimensional Decorations

While the proper treatment of a walking stick's lower end is important, most attention by observers will be directed to details nearer to eye level. Animals particularly draw attention. The public's familiarity with live creatures seems to foster an affinity for reproductions displayed on a stick. Animals carved fully in the round are customary. Mortise and tenon joints and a thin coating of woodworker's glue hold whittlings of this type in place.

The walking stick in Figure 11.9 has been assembled in that way. The mortise was bored into the attachment, and the tenon was whittled to size on the end of the twisted stick.

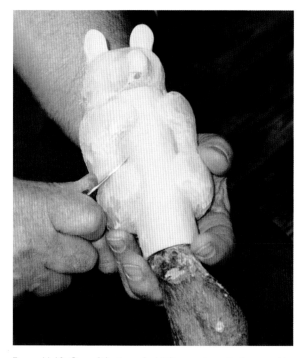

Figure 11.10. One of the joys of whittling creatures in the round is being able to do the work while sitting comfortably in a desirable spot.

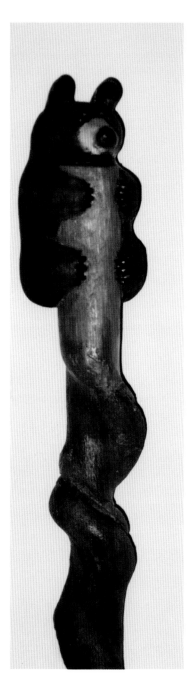

Figure 11.9. This painted, naturalistic carving on a naturally twisted stick meets the recipient's specified requirements.

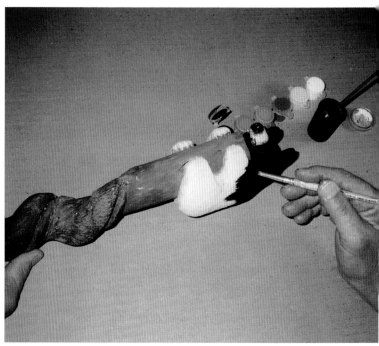

Figure 11.11. Acrylic paint gives the plain basswood carving the realistic appearance desired.

Two conditions were specified by the prospective owner for constructing the article: (1) a black bear was to be carved as if clinging to a pole or tree, and (2) it was to be mounted at the head of a naturally twisted stick of sufficient size for use when walking. The process began by selecting a stick long and stout enough to provide a comfortable handgrip within its spiraled section. The figure of a bear was then shaped for topping the staff. The figure emerged by whittling a block of basswood. As with many three-dimensional pieces, much of the carving was done while sitting in a comfortable location (Figure 11.10). Painting, as shown in progress in Figure 11.11, added the touch of realism needed.

Another animal, this one a stylized version of a Trojan horse's head, decorates a stick in Figure 11.12. Notice the shape of the ears. They are backed up solidly, rather than having a long, thin, more realistic shape that could be broken off easily when hiking. Observe, also, the shape of the handgrip on the lower portion of the pine carving. As previously explained, a properly slanted section enables one to keep a stick generally vertical when walking. It accommodates the natural fold of the clenched hand. The row of slots for fingers add another element of comfort.

Figure 11.12. The small ring in gold and detail painted in red beneath this stylized carving, with its shaped handgrip, is all the color needed.

Should all or part of this carved horse be painted? Designs carved in the style created are best left unpainted. If the wood had a bland or homogeneous grain structure and total realism were intended, the question of coloring might evoke a different response. In this case, the unblemished wood in its natural state and the small amount of red color below the point of attachment are entirely sufficient.

The final carving in the round to be illustrated at this point decorates a walking stick made for an avid fisherman. The assembly appears in Figure 11.13. Below and beyond the pair of naturalistically styled fish lies an area covered with thinly incised lines. Here, again, the line-carved area serves a utilitarian purpose, while the carved fish have no practical value. They are strictly for show. Proficiently applied paint gives a realistic appearance to the basswood carving.

Anyone preparing to fashion a figure in three dimensions, including a stylized version of it, should become familiar with the subject's form through direct observation or by studying illustrations in printed material. The next step would then be to create a drawing of the item as it will be carved. Ordinarily, a line drawing in two views will provide all the detail needed. The sketches in Figure 11.14 are examples. They may be altered in size, shape, and detail to suit individual conditions.

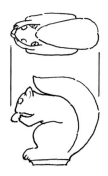

Figure 11.14. Sketches of figures in two outlined views will ordinarily provide sufficient direction for carving animals.

Incised and Relief Designs

Incised and relief-carved shapes also ordinarily originate in some kind of drawing. The design might include a simply carved animal or two, a pattern of repeated floral elements, or an extensive array of geometric shapes. Once established in drawn form, the details can be transferred to or be redrawn onto the surface of the walking stick. Figure 11.15 shows how sparsely outlined these shapes may be for carving in relief.

Figure 11.15. Designs to be carved in relief are often most easily created on bare, round sticks by penciling the shapes in place freehand.

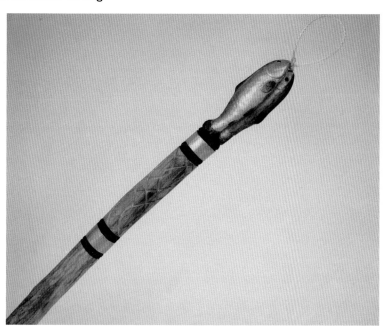

Figure 11.13. Knowledge of a prospective owner's interest is useful in determining what subject, style, and finish will be most admired.

Carving is the next step. Knives and gouges are necessary. The process begins by cutting about the outline of each figure with a sharply pointed flat blade. These incisions serve as stop cuts for the gouging operations. In Figure 11.16, the flowers are made to stand out by texturing the background areas with a gouge. As knowledgeable woodcarvers have learned, good illumination and sidelighting are very helpful when carving such details. On shallow work, they are virtually essential.

Figure 11.16. Light from one side helps provide the shadow and visual acuity sometimes needed when carving in relief.

A walking stick should be completed to the point that painting, if it is to be done, can proceed after carving the decorative forms. Painting will not always be preferred, but it is a definite enhancement on the project in Figure 11.17. The complementary colors applied to the surface being sealed bring out the floral carvings in vivid detail. The entire piece seems to come alive as a consequence of the several applications.

Figure 11.17. Areas of a walking stick painted with acrylics, as well as the unpainted surfaces, should be sealed by a clear finish of some kind.

A design similar to the previous one may be seen in Figure 11.18. A major difference occurs in the way the floral units have been formed. The flower heads in this latest photograph are the result of power incising with a rotary bit. It is a simple and easily duplicated process, partly because the carving can proceed after stripping the bark from only a limited portion of the stick. While interesting in detail, the carving does not produce the degree of realism or provide for firmness in gripping equal to that achieved in relief-carved work.

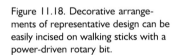

Figure 11.18. Decorative arrangements of representative design can be easily incised on walking sticks with a power-driven rotary bit.

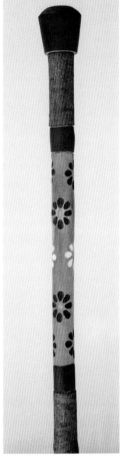

By way of variation, a relief carving of different design covers the walking stick in Figure 11.19. Not all designs in shallow relief must be floral, as this nonrepresentational carving in plane relief shows. The design represents nothing in particular. Made from a birch sapling recovered from a beaver pond in Indian territory (a beaver's tooth marks are still evident on the stick's upper end), the walking stick contains plane-carved features. Limited tool work, a few strips of leather thong, and sparingly applied paint decorate the piece. The lower end of the staff contains a small, compatibly painted carving and a protective tip, as has been recommended for walking sticks of all kinds.

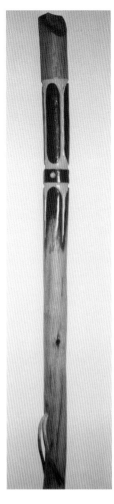

Figure 11.19. Nonrepresentational carvings in plane relief are also applicable in stick work, as this beaver-gnawed birch sapling shows.

from all oviform sections (A) or from only the adjacent areas (B). Also, decisions about color, where to apply it, what hues to apply, or whether to apply any at all, are appropriately made at this point.

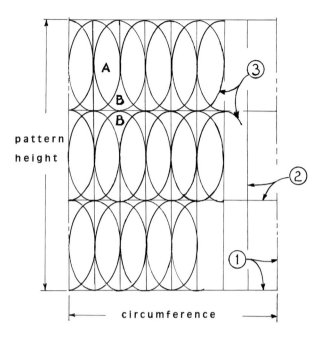

Figure 11.20. This grid for bark carving can be sketched as numbered, with a decision to be made whether to remove bark from sections A or B.

Numerous other variations in relief carving and incising are applicable in the design of walking sticks. These include designs previously shown, such as the diamond pattern illustrated for decorating letter openers, the spiral carving applied in candlestick making, and the chip-carved pattern used to decorate a utensil handle. The stoutness and shape of a stick along its upper part has some bearing on the style and type of decoration that can be accommodated.

Practical Bark Carving

The procedure for carving explained in this section is, as noted before, a form of relief carving. Its features are similar to those in plane carving. A major difference, and an extremely important one, is the use of wood with tightly clinging bark in the applications currently under consideration. Anyone planning to make a bark-covered walking stick should select a branch or sapling that has not only both the inner and outer bark intact, but also one having a comparatively smooth surface. Pieces having very rough, loose, or scaly surfaces will not do.

As usual, the design work begins with sketching. A procedure for drawing one form of pattern is given in Figure 11.20. Several different arrangements might be sketched at this stage. The process begins by determining and marking off the stick's perimeter and the design's intended height. The designer then must determine not only the size, shape, and number of cells most suitable for the decoration, but also the areas of the pattern from which the stick's bark will eventually be removed. Two different applications can be obtained from each pattern drawn. In the sketch shown, the bark may be removed either

The chosen design must be transferred in some manner to the walking stick. Redrawing the pattern directly on the stick will often be the preferred way. To do that, one simply reconstructs the layout on the bark by following the order identified in the sketch. This process is shown in Figure 11.21. The use of a felt-tip pen produces the darkness of lines needed for carving. Penciled lines seldom provide enough contrast on bark. To avoid having the inked line work show permanently, all such marks in patterns intended for finishing in the natural must be carved away. Doing that might alter the shapes somewhat. The problem can be completely ignored when the elevated portions of an inked pattern are to be covered with paint.

Figure 11.21. A felt-tip pen will usually produce the intensity needed, but any lines left on the bark after carving must be covered by paint.

The carving process involves the use of a knife, first for incising along the drawn outlines and, secondly, for cutting away selected parts of the bark. The incised lines are essential for removing bark cleanly. In this process, the woodcarver will often be faced with a choice about the depth of carving. A frequent decision is whether to cut away only the outer bark, leaving the brownish inner bark stand, or whether to remove both layers clear to the lighter sapwood within. The decision may hinge on the appearance desired, although the inner bark on some saplings will be found to be too soft and porous for leaving exposed. Both layers of bark are shown being removed in Figure 11.22.

Figure 11.22. Whether to remove both outer and inner bark from chosen sections depends on the thickness, color, and firmness obtainable and desired.

Figure 11.23 presents a view of the carved stick being painted. Obviously, the selection of colors leaves the way open for considerable variety in such applications. Several alternatives may be seen by referring to the bark-carved sticks presented earlier in this chapter.

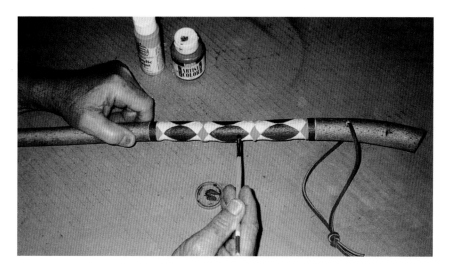

Figure 11.23. The color on the bark in the carved area is a visual enhancement, while the leather loop might be used for hanging and holding.

The looped leather thong on the stick has been placed there for purposes of utility, yet it might be an unessential addition. Its placement is proper for supporting one's hand when walking, but some individuals will undoubtedly grip only the carved section while on a stroll. Another possible use for the loop is hanging. The value of this feature seems evident. Nevertheless, not all walkers are likely to store a stick by attaching its leather loop to a hook. Some will prefer to prop the piece out of the way in a closet or in a corner of a room. The message for the designer is clear: Whenever possible, determine the preferences of the person who will use the creation you are planning.

Carving Colorful Canes

Utility is undoubtedly the primary concern in the design of canes. They must be strong, have an easily gripped handhold, be of the exact length needed by an individual for support, and have a tip covered with a material that will neither slip on slick surfaces nor snag threads in carpets and rugs. In many instances, carved details are applied for decorative purposes, but carving will occasionally provide some practical assistance when applied to a handgrip. Examples occur in which the roots of small trees having the form of a cane's handle have been carved smooth. Figure 11.24 illustrates this. The cane's handle has a naturally utilitarian form, without having required much carving and sanding.

Figure 11.24. A cane's handle, when formed from the root of a sapling, will sometimes be more practical than esthetic.

The cane in Figure 11.25 contains a carving that is only minimally utilitarian. The tooled eagle's head is there mainly for appearance. This naturally grown handle would function about as well without the carved feature as with it.

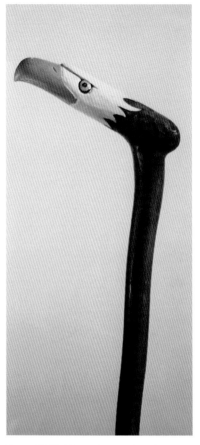

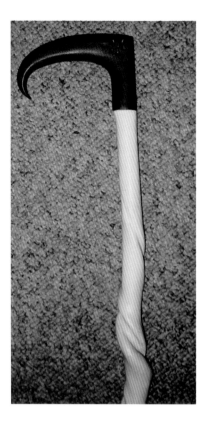

Figure 11.26. A handle carved from walnut crotch wood, while somewhat difficult to carve, makes a strong and durable piece.

Figure 11.25. The eagle carved on this naturally grown cane head is an example of applying a design according to what the piece will accommodate.

The handgrip shown in Figure 11.26, by way of comparison, has been completely structured by hand. Both the shape of the piece and the small, incised figures on each side have been carved. In order to assure adequacy of strength, figured crotch wood was selected for the walnut handle, and a four-inch steel rod was inserted to reinforce the joint attaching the piece to the twisted stick. Also, the assembly was sized in length to that needed by a particular individual, with slip-resistant plastic covering the cane's tip. Bark on the cane was replaced with paint, as may be evident in Figure 11.27.

Figure 11.27. The finished cane shown here has been sized to length for a particular individual before painting and covering the tip at the bottom.

The several examples presented here further illustrate the design and application of carving to useful items. Were a woodcarver so inclined, he or she could spend a lifetime doing nothing more than creating walking sticks and canes of different configuration. It is another phase of the craft that seems to have no limit.

Chapter Twelve
Lettering Nameplates and Signs

Woodcarvers are occasionally faced with a need to apply letters and numbers in their work. The practice can hardly be avoided by those devoted to carving items of practical value. Hobbyists, especially those who develop an affinity for things pragmatic, are likely to apply lettering to such things as nameplates, house numbers, and welcome signs, and professional sign makers who have the ability to design and carve alphabets proficiently are constantly in demand for their skills. All must know which of the many available styles of lettering will provide the legibility and prominence needed. They must also be cognizant of the manner of execution appropriate for carving the letters in the style selected.

Lettering exists in many styles, and new ones emerge continually. Many are readily available. Office supply and craft stores often carry sheets of transfer-type alphabets, libraries commonly stock books on lettering, and most computers are equipped with alphabets that can be brought up with the click of a mouse. Some books contain information on proportioning the different characters in their capital and lower-case forms, while computers will produce underlined, italicized, bold, or regular alphabets in dozens of different styles and point sizes.

Incised and Relief Lettering

Although the styles of lettering and numbering seem limitless in variety, each and every one can be created in wood by selectively applying the methods of incising and relief carving. Some alphabets can be carved by either method, but others are more easily and appropriately carved by one method or the other. Letters standing in relief above a background generally require broad elements, but some letters have extremely small or narrow parts. Incising is then usually preferred. If made in relief, tiny letters and those having thin sections would likely be weak and easily broken off. Many letters carved in relief are sans serif for that reason.

The letters incised in the weathered-wood plaque (Figure 12.1) illustrate a style that would have been neither appropriate or easily carved in relief. The thinness of elements and softness of the wood, rather than the expanse of lettering in "Welcome," dictated the method of carving to be used. Besides, there was a desire to leave much of the weathered surface on the 5 1/2 x 24-inch board visible. Relief carving would have taken away more of the surface for the background. The intent was to produce lettering in a clean, unpainted, formal style that would reveal the underlying wood and contrast nicely with the rustic board. The incised, floral figures to the sides were painted to further accentuate the message.

Figure 12.1. The incised lettering and painted floral figures contrast effectively with the weathered surface in this homespun greeting.

Welcome signs have become very popular, and those made of weathered wood seem to have acquired special appeal. Something similar to the one shown would make a good project for a beginner's first effort at carving letters.

Whenever the carving of a set of letters can be done either in relief or by incising, the choice of which to use depends more on the suitability for conveying the message than on a practical limitation of the carving method. How effectively the lettering will communicate the meaning intended becomes the criterion of most concern. Legibility plays a substantial, if not a dominate, role in the matter.

Aptness of style is also important. The shapes of letters must not detract from the mood desired. Numerous examples could be given. A haphazard, whimsical style of lettering, for example, would not be appropriate for a serious piece such as a directional sign. The same thing can be said about using an old English style where a less-ornate Gothic or Roman form would be better. The lettering of a welcome sign in weathered wood is an example.

In some instances, any of several different styles of lettering could be used on a particular item. At other times, an object will seem to dictate the style of lettering and manner of carving to be used. The carved mahogany emblem in Figure 12.2 suggests the type. The piece symbolizes an award given to a college student for achievement and subsequent acceptance into an academic fraternity. The Greek letters (Iota, Lambda, Sigma) are in relief, as seems only appropriate and in keeping with the carving of the other details. The plane faces on the letters stand in contrast and provide a measure of prominence in the scheme.

Figure 12.2. The plane surfaces on the Greek Letters in this academic fraternity emblem stand out prominently among the relief-carved details.

Nameplates and Tags

Proportion and spacing are concerns when lettering. Analysis of the shapes of letters in printed material will reveal the relative horizontal and vertical dimensions of each letter. Spacing is somewhat more difficult to master, as there are no easily applied measurements. Linear measurement does not apply at all. The area between letters counts most, and those areas must be kept equal for best appearance. Because of the many possible combinations of adjacent characters in writing, some acuity becomes necessary to achieve a balanced distribution within and between words. The number of letters in a work makes no difference. Letters in a short name must be spaced by eye just as those in long messages require proportionate spacing. Both capital and lower-case letters require this treatment.

A nameplate lettered in capitals is shown in Figure 12.3. The Tristan style of lettering forms the name. Notice that the serifs are substantial in size.

Figure 12.4. Letters of adequate size and spacing—these in Tristan style were generated by computer—are needed for viewing from a distance.

Figure 12.3. Although readability is the primary concern for a nameplate, letters that are not too plain or common in shape add interest to the piece.

The basic requirements of a nameplate, which will ordinarily rest on a desk for viewing by persons approaching, are legibility and prominence. The name must stand out enough to be easily read. Thus, the size of the piece shown—this one being 2 1/8 x 2 3/8 x 8 1/4 inches—is large enough to contain letters that can be easily viewed from a distance. The size and extended spacing of the letters and the slanted surface into which they have been carved contribute to their prominence. Gold on the flat surfaces of the letters also accounts for much visibility. It contrasts markedly with the redness of the cherry wood.

The style of lettering chosen has much to do with the name's legibility. The style used may be described as "clean." In other words, it is not so ornate as to be difficult to determine what each character represents. Moreover, the simple, comparatively bold form used is more masculine than would be, say, lettering in script. Yet, the style carved into the nameplate incorporates enough variation in the individual shapes to avoid the monotony of some sans serif alphabets.

The construction of a nameplate, as has been emphasized repeatedly for other articles, precedes the carving. Insofar as possible, all shaping and sanding should be done first. The next step is to sketch or trace the previously sketched design onto the surface to be carved, as in Figure 12.4.

The carving operation begins by incising along each letter's outline with a flat blade. The depth need only be about 1/8 inch to provide stop cuts for removing the surrounding wood to a shallow depth. The use of a gouge, driven by a mallet, is recommended for much of this operation in the cherry wood (Figure 12.5). A square-nose tool can be used to advantage for removing wood adjacent to the letters.

Figure 12.5. Carving involves incising about each letter's outline, gouging background wood to a shallow depth, and stippling the carved surfaces.

The final step in tooling a nameplate as illustrated is stippling, a procedure which, if done carefully in random fashion, will provide a comparatively uniform appearance in low relief. A common nail may be reshaped on either of its two ends for this purpose. By using the pointed end, stippling can be done in tight areas and corners, but a considerable amount of tapping will be necessary to tool the entire background evenly. If, on the other hand, the circular head of the nail is grooved in a crisscross pattern, the stippling can proceed faster, but then the narrow spaces will have to be stippled another way and there is danger of obtaining a spotty pattern of impressions from the nail head. That result could be more of a distraction than an enhancement. Use of a reshaped, pointed end of a nail throughout the background will often give a better result.

The finish applied to a nameplate also has much to do with appearance. In this case (Figure 12.6), boiled linseed oil was rubbed into the surface to bring out the carving and the redness of the cherry wood. The oil was allowed to penetrate and dry for several days before spraying on satin polyurethane and painting the surfaces of letters (Figure 12.7). Gold acrylic paint was chosen for the elegance it connotes.

Figure 12.6. Boiled linseed oil brings out the redness of cherry wood, which can be sealed with a clear finish when thoroughly dry.

Figure 12.7. Acrylic paint in vividly contrasting color, applied between coats of polyurethane, creates the prominence desired in a nameplate.

A nameplate of another design may be observed in Figure 12.8. Its overall dimensions are 1 7/8 x 6 x 4 inches. The pieces making up the assembly are 3/8 inch and 5/8 inch cherry wood. Obviously made for a woman, the delicate lettering can be easily read by virtue of its size, contrast, and use on a slanted surface.

Figure 12.8. Lettering is preferably done in a style appropriate for the gender of the person on whose desk the nameplate will be placed.

Designed for incising, a pattern of the configuration shown is most easily carved with a blade of the proper shape. A flat blade with a curved cutting edge and sharply pointed tip works especially well. The one shown in use in Figure 12.9 will cleanly incise tight curves better than tools with wide blades.

Figure 12.9. A hooked blade with a sharp point is especially useful for incising sharp curves in a wood as firm as cherry.

Prominence and ease of recognition of the name are essential in this version, too. For that reason, black paint was applied in the grooves of the lettering (Figure 12.10). In order to avoid having the paint bleed into the wood, a coat of polyurethane was first sprayed over the surface and allowed to dry. This coating also protected the wood from paint spread outside the incised grooves. The unwanted excesses, which often occurred while brushing, were readily removed with a knife blade. A light sanding of the surface also helped clean the surface preparatory to a final application of satin polyurethane.

Figure 12.10. Acrylic paint should be applied over a dry coat of clear sealer to prevent the acrylic from bleeding into surrounding wood.

The name tag shown in Figure 12.11 has also been developed with special considerations of prominence, readability, and construction in mind. This object contains a pin on its back for attaching to an individual's shirt or coat lapel. As in the previous example, the name and other parts were incised, but both the name on the tag and the chip-carved details forming the border were painted in black, though in different intensity. The leaf-like border was designed so that the details would "read" upright regardless of the angle from which viewed. The precision required in carving a name tag of similar design has been captured in Figure 12.12.

Figure 12.12. The floral details in the chip-carved border are designed to appear upright, whether viewed from one angle or another.

Figure 12.13. A plaque carved in this design, when placed on the desk of someone with a sense of humor, could be just what your workplace needs.

The 1/4 x 2 1/8 x 3 3/8-inch name tag was constructed from cherry wood. The main reason it had been chosen is durability, a matter of importance for wooden objects subject to considerable handling and some wear. The wood's color was a second reason.

Special Applications

Lettering adds a dimension to some carved work which, by itself, would not fully convey the meaning intended. Consider something humorous, for instance. A half-round carving of a frazzled rooster tugging on a worm, actually a heavy string, could be funny if given visibility on a plaque. However, carve "Do I have to get up this early?" beside the frantically struggling bird and a whole new aspect of humor emerges. Put your mind to the task and you will probably come up with funnier arrangements. For sure, that could be difficult. As a comedian once said, being funny is no laughing matter.

Humor brings forth laughter, and laughter is good for the soul. Do you have a boss who has a sense of humor, or do you have a desk job that has not been hidden away in some not-often-frequented corner? Consider, in any case, preparing a plaque with a message for standing on a desk. A carved figure and incised wording similar to that in Figure 12.13 just might provide the light atmosphere needed in your workplace. The moments of hilarity bursting from those who "get it" could be well worth the effort.

Messages can be presented in a style of lettering suitable for nearly any mood or purpose. Therein lies a strength. Frivolous, serious, chaotic, elegant, and stoic representations are a few possibilities. The purpose of the item is paramount in determining what the style shall be. By way of illustration, a wooden cover on one's personal album of photographs might be provided with lettering similar to that in Figure 12.14. The carving of such letters, being most suitable for relief carving, assumes a modern, casual form of identifying the album's purpose is preferred to others. A very formal style might be preferred by some individuals, for more than a single style will sometimes serve the purpose.

Figure 12.14. A modern alphabet in the form shown is designed exclusively for carving in plane relief.

House and Community Signs

Signs containing house numbers and those identifying the names of housing developments are commonly seen today. They are ideal for carving, especially if something a bit out of the ordinary is desired. Each location can be given a unique identifier, and each sign can be customized to meet individual needs and preferences. While the numbers and letters fashioned in wood must meet the requirements of legibility, the carved details accompanying them may follow any of many avenues.

Figure 12.15 contains a practical example. The house number is clear and easily read from the street out front. The remaining part of the design is decorative. Why a floral design was added to the plaque is simply the result of the woodcarver interpreting what the owner wanted. It does add an element of variety and interest, yet it does not dominate or in some way detract from the plaque's purpose.

Figure 12.15. A carved plaque on a house can exhibit an individuality not obtainable by ordinary methods of house numbering.

Carved in relief, the pine plaque shows gouge marks on the surface in the background. This method of detailing represents an alternative to stippling. It is often used in some form in areas where the wood will be finished in the natural. Oil paints and an exterior grade of satin polyurethane protect the work.

Successful sign makers are experts at customizing work. They have learned that progress professionally depends on an ability to design items individually and make each a practical work of art. Functionality, in all cases, becomes the guiding objective.

A sign, the work of a highly qualified professional, identifies a particular housing development in Figure 12.16. Both the design and the material are special. The carver has produced a visual image in keeping with the wording, with the entire piece being comprised of Spanish cedar. The wood is special, in that, it was once commonly used by boat builders for its durability when subjected to water and weathering. It also takes paint well.

Figure 12.16. This sign reveals the woodcarver's ability to create an easily read, attractive, and relevant identification for a particular community.

This woodcarver's ability to relate his designs to the situation at hand, as well as to do the work skillfully, has been verified by the fact that in the past 20 years he has produced nearly 800 custom signs—all of which were commissioned without formal advertising. Word of mouth alone contributed to his success. The demand for his business signs and house emblems has continued to increase in recent years.

Business Signs

Another sign by the creator of the sign at Mallard Ponds may be seen in Figure 12.18. This sign has an elegance and sophistication that is a further indication of the professional quality of his creations. Both the incised lettering and the relief-carved features are neatly done. Except for the stained wood, gold leaf covers all surfaces. The gold leaf, which is said to have a life of 30 or more years under weather, covers the carved elements completely. Appearance and protection are the reasons for its use.

A close-up view reveals the types of carving the designer used in the item. The ducks are carved half-round and mounted as appliques, and the lettering is incised in Roman style for maximum readability. These features are evident in Figures 12.17. What seems less obvious is the use of gold leaf in the lettering and on the finials topping the posts. Used is 23-karat gold leaf, a hammered foil of metallic gold.

Figure 12.17. Ducks in relief, Roman letters deeply incised, durably painted Spanish cedar, and gold leaf are used effectively to convey the message.

Figure 12.18. Also carved by the creator of the Mallard Ponds project, this sign further indicates the high level of skill achieved.

A sign made by a different woodcarver is presented in Figure 12.19. Its style and construction are different, too. The piece has been made for hanging in an area protected from weathering at a seaside establishment. It is 3/4 x 14 x 24 inches in size, made of pine wood, and hand-carved, except for the rope strips which are machine-carved moldings. How the features relate to the lettered name are worthy of noting. The background in blue, the lifelike carved applique of a dolphin breaching, and the rope border, exhibit an aura of compatibility with the stylized lettering. How the name stands out so prominently, even though carved in bas-relief, also helps satisfy design requirements. The relationship achieved among the several elements in this comparatively simple application brings out a point of significance. The reinforcement the items provide each other is something to be observed in the development of business signs of all kinds.

The final example of sign work to be shown here, a sign on the face of an office building for a physician, is presented in Figure 12.20. The symbol and the doctor's name are carved in relief. Lacking the protection of stain or paint, the fir wood shows signs of deteriorating.

Figure 12.19. The name on this indoor sign is reinforced by an association of features—a dolphin breaching, a rope border, and the blue color.

Figure 12.20. Carved in relief, this sign still conveys the message clearly, even though the unprotected wood has begun to deteriorate.

Chapter Thirteen
Fashioning Useful Miscellanea

This final chapter covers the design and carving of items which, with one or two exceptions, are personally oriented. Decorative brooches, bolo ties, back-scratchers, key-chain attachments, chess pieces, and business-card holders constitute most of the applications. Also explained and illustrated is a little-used method of carving. It is applicable to household articles as well as to some made for personal use.

Apparel Accessories

The opportunities for being creative are extensive for anyone who devotes attention to the design and carving of articles for use with wearing apparel. Brooches and bolo ties are particularly popular. They have become so popular, in fact, that many craft and wood-carving supply houses keep brooch pins, braided tie cords, and tie slides available in several varieties.

Within limits, individual preferences largely determine the design of the wooden part of the accessories. Almost any style and method of carving can be used, including carving in the round, bas-relief, and chip carving. Shape and bulk are among the physical limitations of concern, with excessive weight, sharp points, and fragile parts definitely to be avoided on accessories made for use on or near garments. Otherwise, the opportunities for creative expression freely abound.

Some freedom in design may be seen in the asymmetrical pattern of incised stars on the wooden part of a bolo tie in Figure 13.1. The ovoid section of wood is pawpaw. The face of the 5/16 x 1 3/4 x 2 1/2-inch piece has a slight curvature, but the back is flat. Gold paint in the chip-carved figures augments their visibility. Clear polyurethane over both the painted and unpainted surfaces provides the finishing touch. As to appearance, the design of the piece avoids the rigidity inherent in some formally balanced, symmetrical distributions.

Pawpaw wood is uniquely colorful. It also has a soft texture. Because of its texture, pawpaw does not carve as cleanly as firmer woods. Its tendency to chip and crush while carving can be overcome to a considerable extent by applying a thin solution of polyurethane. A mixture of 1/3 polyurethane and 2/3 mineral spirits will penetrate as desired. When dry, the wood will have a firmness that makes carving comparatively easy. Staining, thereafter, no longer remains a desirable option—in case anyone would consider coloring the naturally greenish wood.

The incising of the piece for the bolo after treating it as suggested may be seen in Figure 13.2. Sidelighting provides the shadows helpful for precise carving. Any penciled lines left on the surface after carving can be removed by sanding. This assumes, of course, that the wood has not been deeply grooved by the pencil point.

Figure 13.2. A light placed to one side is virtually essential for viewing the work while incising the dark wood.

During the painting process (Figure 13.3), the spreading of acrylic onto adjacent surfaces can scarcely be avoided. Complete removal of any overflow is possible by scraping and sanding, provided that a sealer has been applied beforehand to prevent bleeding into the wood. Would paint of another color be as effective as gold for this article? A shiny silver might be a good alternative. It would seem to enhance the wood just as effectively as the gold does.

Figure 13.1. The asymmetrically arranged decoration in this bolo tie makes an interesting contrast with the naturally finished pawpaw wood.

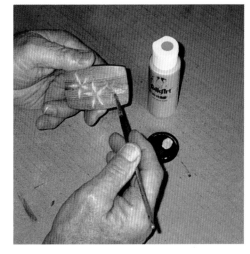

Figure 13.3. Polyurethane applied to the surface and allowed to dry prior to painting will make possible complete removal of any overflow of acrylic.

Figure 13.4 is a photograph of a more ornately carved bolo tie. The craftsman who created this piece is expert at power carving and adding fine detail with a burning tool. He also prefers to use tupelo for its strength and capacity for holding sharp detail. His preferences are embodied in the conventionalized arrangement shown.

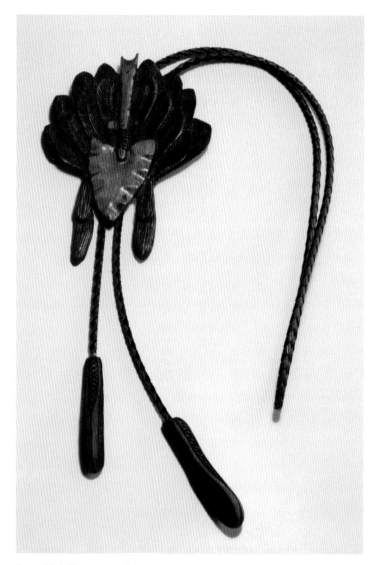

Figure 13.4. The creator of this bolo tie used a wood burning tool to detail the feathers in the symmetrical spread.

This same craftsman has an ability to represent wildlife naturalistically, as is apparent in his brooches. Examples are presented in Figure 13.5. His skill in carving small birds, burning and coloring the figures realistically, and fashioning them half-round for practical use is evident. Some of the steps in constructing the brooches may be seen in Figure 13.6. It pictures a blank sawed for carving a pheasant and the back of a duck cutout with a pin attached. His work epitomizes the level of perfection a retiree might achieve just for the fun of it. The work is also an excellent model for persons interested in duplicating natural form.

Figure 13.5. Skill in carving and painting wildlife as realistically as the creatures appear in nature is evident in the small brooches shown here.

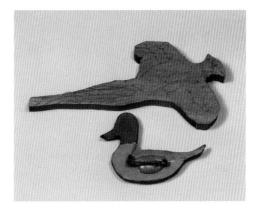

Figure 13.6. Several steps in making brooches are indicated by the cutout blank of a ring-neck and the back of a carved red-head with pin attached.

People who desire to create designs, rather than emulate something, are sometimes oriented toward the abstract. Abstraction provides boundless opportunities for expression. A creation might be a nonrepresentational figure of complex form or one as simple as that in Figure 13.7. The degree of complexity involved has little to do with artistic quality. Personal preferences often vary independently, as well.

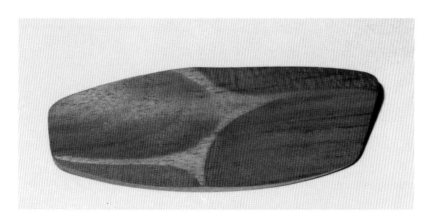

Figure 13.7. In contrast to realistic designs, this abstract brooch draws appeal from the wood's beauty and distributions of line, mass, and form.

The brooch illustrated is 7/8 x 2 5/8 inches overall, with a maximum thickness of 3/8-inch. It is made of walnut wood, finished with a matte coat of polyurethane, and has a pin attached to the back for fastening to a dress. What does this carved piece represent? Absolutely nothing. The combination of elements within the piece are intended to create visual interest on their own. The beauty of the wood is one thing. Other features defining artistic merit are the brooch's lines and form created by sawing, gouging, and sanding.

Other Personal-Use Items

Back-scratchers offer still more opportunities for individual creativity, but they, too, embody specific limitations. Aspects of design may vary insofar as a device's length, handgrip, and scratching tip fulfill practical needs. A section of a 1-inch tree branch about 18 inches long will do. One having a slight curvature is good for reaching across a shoulder.

That shown in Figure 13.8 satisfies the basic requirements. It does so especially well as a consequence of the inner bark having been left for shaping into a handgrip and having provided a projection on the other end for scratching an itch. The leather loop attached to the handle serves the function of hanging. The paint serves a decorative purpose while lending character to the mythological creature represented on the itch-scratching end. The wood is willow. How nicely it carves is indicated somewhat by the detail in the close-up, Figure 13.9.

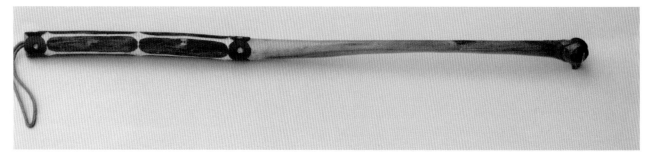

Figure 13.8. A back-scratcher whittled from a willow branch can be as unusual as it is effective for "eating" itches.

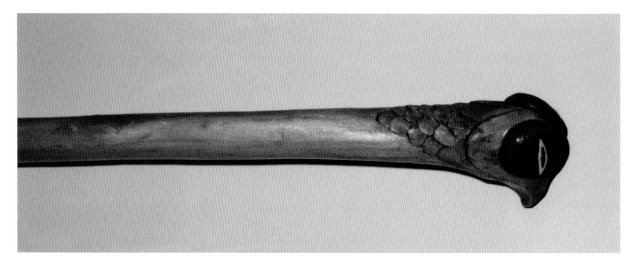

Figure 13.9. A close-up of the itch eater's head shows what a bit of precise carving and paint will achieve.

Representational forms can be readily adapted to back-scratchers. Eagle claws, boar tusks, and rake teeth represent only a few alternative shapes that could satisfy persons with a penchant for things realistic.

The scratcher shown in Figure 13.10 is a multi-representational device, being covered with a hodgepodge of shapes and colors. The scratcher is essentially a doodle stick, in that, unrelated items are combined. A serpent, geometric shapes, and totem-like figures are represented. The ovoid shapes on the rod are similar to the elements favored by Northwest Indians in their designs, and the cobra is an animal from a different part of the world. These incongruities matter little in this relief-carved conglomeration. Perhaps, the liberal use of paint will satisfy those who like colorful decorations. Seemingly more decorative than practical, the colorful stick does, nevertheless, contain a small metal nail which has been rounded for use in scratching. While serving that purpose adequately, a back-scratcher made with a tip of this kind should be kept out of reach of young children.

In this application (Figure 13.11), a horse's head 9/16-inch thick by nearly 2 inches across decorates the article. The wood is sugar pine. Its homogeneous grain carves easily (Figure 13.12). The details are carved on both sides of the head. A clear, matte finish eventually covers the piece without first having applied stain or paint of any kind.

Figure 13.11. The head of a horse carved and "epoxied" in place on this key chain seems far superior to the plastic attachment it replaced.

Figure 13.10. This colorful back-scratcher has an incongruous combination of figures of geometric, East Indian, and Northwest Indian influence.

Woodcarvers who are oriented to whittling objects in the round may find this next application to their liking. As with the apparel accessories illustrated earlier, the carved figure has a metal attachment—this one a chain and ring for holding keys. A three-dimensional whittling can be fixed and epoxied to a link to complete the key chain. The whittling need not be large, but it should not be so fragile as to be easily damaged. Chains and rings of different sizes can be purchased for making the utilitarian devices. An alternative practice is to remove the plastic attachment from an inexpensive assembly and replace it with a carved decoration. The choice of subject for the replacement seems to be virtually unlimited for a person with ability to do the carving.

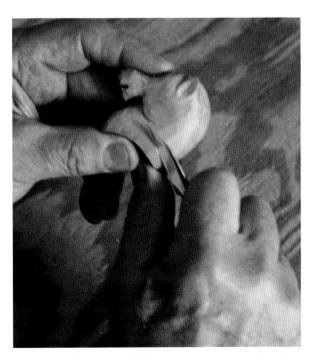

Figure 13.12. The soft wood of the sugar pine being carved for the key chain is as easily tooled as basswood.

Articles made by woodcarving can serve purposes of various types, whether serious, casual, humorous, or frivolous, etc. A chess set is one made for serious, leisure-time use. Part of a set is shown in Figure 13.13. The pieces are intended for individual use when playing against the electronic board on which they stand.

Figure 13.13. Another effective use of carving is the final shaping of several major pieces in a turned chess set.

To make a set as shown, each piece is first turned on a lathe. Only parts of some pieces are shaped that way, as certain details must be finished by carving. The knight involves the most carving. This can be a challenge. Achieving uniformity among pieces of the same design requires skill and care, but when completed, the result can be an individualized creation not obtainable in comparable form commercially.

Chess, certainly, is not the only game that might incorporate carved features. Practically any plaything constructed in wood can be decorated by carving some part of it. Checkers carved in relief and cribbage boards containing incised designs are two other possibilities in which desirable results are obtainable. The designs applicable are left to the designer's imagination.

For Those in Charge

Anyone appointed or elected to lead a club or civic organization will find a gavel to be indispensable at meetings. Members everywhere have come to respect the authority it represents. A mallet made of firm wood, with a plate for striking to match, could be exactly what your group needs. Make a pair for the group's leader or for your own personal use while in charge. Add a special, decorative touch by carving the two pieces, but be sure to keep the style compatible throughout.

An individually crafted pair is presented in Figure 13.14. Both pieces are constructed of walnut wood. The strike-plate, a piece an inch thick and 4 3/4 inches in diameter, contains a circular design surrounding an uncarved central area for striking. The mallet is 10 inches long, its head is 2 inches in diameter by 3 3/8 inches in length, and the handle at the end carved for gripping is about 1 1/8 inches thick. The designs on the mallet and plate are placed in positions where damage from striking will not be likely. They are incised for the same reason. Figures in relief, especially if carved on the visible surface of the strike plate, would not hold up as well from use as the incised patterns.

Figure 13.14. A gavel and strike-plate made of walnut wood and decorated by incising is one more example of enhancing a useful project by carving.

For convenience, parts of the walnut gavel have been turned on a lathe before decorating. That method of production is not totally essential, however. A variety of different shapes can be made by carving. In any case, the woodcarver who takes pride in his or her finished creation should sign the work. A small symbol made in the manner of the trademarks so commonly used on individually crafted pieces in years past is suggested. A representative design carved on the bottom of the strike plate would be appropriate.

A useful article of another kind is the card holder. People having reason to promote something will often create 2 x 3 1/2-inch business cards of attractive design. Some will display their cards on desks or tables in small wooden holders that can be easily seen and be readily accessed by potential clients or customers. A specially designed and personally carved holder could provide the eye-catching appeal desired.

To be special a card holder does not have to be elaborate—just different. An infrequently used method of edge carving might do all that can be expected. A particularly easy method to apply, the beveling of edges in undulating curves makes a simple but attractive design.

An edge-carved card holder, an assembly 1 1/2 x 4 1/4 x 2 3/4 inches overall, supports a pack of business cards in Figure 13.15. The uprights are 1/4-inch pine, and the base is pine of 1/2-inch thickness. The angle of presentation built in by slanting the rear piece backward satisfies the requirements of ease in viewing and removing cards.

Figure 13.15. A decorative border carved along the edges of a business card holder lends an element of individuality to the cards and their purpose.

The carving along the edge is the result of beveling with a knife at an angle of 45 degrees. Figure 13.16 shows the process in progress.

Figure 13.16. The carving of edges on a 45-degree bevel can be done on thin pieces by whittling with a flat blade.

The design along the front edges is a combination of cyma curves. Their rhythmically flowing quality is evident. They are inherently flexible as regards length and number of curves in a sequence, making them convenient for decorating edges of different thicknesses and lengths.

Edge-Carving Applications

Although decorating by carving a surface's edges on a bevel may be applied to articles of many kinds, applications along horizontal lines in valences, shelves, and cabinets are especially attractive. The method is a particularly good substitute for the scalloped edges carpenters in years past sometimes sawed along the horizontal members of such items. Beveled-edge carvings are substantial. Not as much wood must be removed as occurs when scalloping by sawing, leaving the edges stronger and less likely to have pieces broken off.

Part of the edge-carved trim board on a closet shelf has been captured in Figure 13.17. For the sake of appearance, the carved details have been terminated a short distance from the ends of the strip. Also, the curved units were adjusted in length to cover the distance to be carved with units of full and equal dimensions.

Figure 13.17. The decorative edge on the trim of a closet shelf is indicative of what can be achieved by this method of carving.

The layout for such carving can be done uniformly with a properly designed template. Only one section of the pattern must be drawn and cut along the curve created. That section can be turned over repeatedly as necessary for tracing the entire series of curves in a design (Figure 13.18). Of importance to notice is the depth of curvature. The size of the curvature on the template and on the board's surface must equal the board's thickness in order to achieve a 45-degree bevel. Any other angle would serve no beneficial purpose.

Figure 13.18. The easiest way to draw a pattern uniformly is with a template shaped to provide 45-degree bevels and full units along a board's edge.

Saw cuts of two kinds are involved in this form of carving: those for the straight lines in a design and those acting as stop cuts and for gauging depth when chiseling the concavely curved sections (Figure 13.19). Care must be exercised to avoid sawing too deep. Sawing into the back surface of the board could ruin the decoration.

Figure 13.19. A backsaw is useful for cutting the straight parts of a pattern and for making depth and stop cuts in the areas to be carved.

The next step is carving. A flat chisel is used, as in Figure 13.20. One that reaches clear across the beveled surface is best for making straight cuts and controlling depth of cut. As with excessive sawing, gouging too deep could ruin appearance. Slight sanding may be desirable after completing the carved work. For another application of this type of carving, the reader should refer to the pierced wall shelf pictured in Chapter 9. The center section contains the edge carving.

The applications in this chapter, as in the earlier presentations, are examples of decorative carving applied to useful products. Hopefully, the different examples will contribute to the broad edification of woodcarvers and to the useful application of the methods involved.

Figure 13.20. The chisel used for creating the decoration should be flat and wide enough to extend across the carved bevel at its widest point.

Index